The Maiden Voyage of the Charlotte Jane 1848 – 50

DESCRIBED BY MIRIAM LAWRENCE AND CAPTAIN ALEXANDER LAWRENCE

COMPILED BY

CASS MOGGRIDGE

Grosvenor House
Publishing Limited

This book is published by
Grosvenor House Publishing Ltd
Link House
140 The Broadway, Tolworth, Surrey, KT6 7HT.
www.grosvenorhousepublishing.co.uk

A CIP record for this book
is available from the British Library

ISBN 978-1-83975-495-1

DEDICATION

Miriam Lawrence wrote her memoir for her grandchildren. I would like to dedicate this book to our grandchildren. Joseph, Henry, Anna and Zoe

CONTENTS

ACKNOWLEDGEMENTS

This has been a long time in the making and many people have helped me over the years. My husband, Hal Moggridge, has joined in from the beginning, deciphering difficult words in the memoir and log book, commenting on different versions of the text, drawing all the maps that show each stage of the voyage, as well as collecting and assembling the illustrations. Thank you, Hal, for your steady presence and encouragement and the fun we have had.

Special thanks to Dr Helen Doe for reading the text and providing invaluable information and comments.

Thanks to the Canterbury Museum, Christchurch, New Zealand, particularly Sarah Murray and Julia Bradbury; and to Phyl and Mike Thorpe who visited the Museum while on holiday in New Zealand, and brought back valuable information and photos.

To all my family, Harriet, Joseph, Henry, Geoffrey, Lawrence, Karin, Eric, Alex Moggridge, Nicholas Lawrence, (Not related to Miriam and Alexander,) Liana Chua, Juliana Lim. Many thanks to you all for your interest, encouragement, patience, and practical help in so many different ways.

Thanks to Sheila Pregnall and Peter Webber for reading the text and commenting; to Sue Greenwood for helping me adapt to Apple; to Pat Grover for help at the start.

I am grateful to Grosvenor House Publishing for working so hard through this pandemic when so many people have wanted to publish a book!

INTRODUCTION

When clearing out our attic I found an old suitcase that had belonged to my mother-in-law. I took it downstairs for Hal, my husband and I to sort out. It was full of old photos, some beautiful flower drawings and two exercise books which were extremely difficult to read. Eventually we realised that they both contained almost identical versions of a memoir written by Hal's great grandmother Miriam Lawrence. They tell the story of the maiden voyage of the sailing ship the *Charlotte Jane* in 1848 on which at the age of 20, she accompanied her husband, the ship's master, Captain Alexander Lawrence. They took with them their 6½-month-old baby daughter, Harriet and a young girl to help with child care. The writing is almost indecipherable but I learned to read it. The words leapt off the page and I became utterly engrossed.

We then discovered that we had the log book of the same voyage written by Captain Lawrence himself. His writing is even more illegible! However, Hal has made maps drawn to scale of each passage of the voyage using the daily longitude and latitude readings from the log book. There are also some letters from and to Alexander and Miriam and her parents. They too are difficult to read as they are written on both sides of very thin paper with further writing at right angles in-between the lines.

Miriam first met Alexander at her aunt's house in London. Thirteen months later they married. She was 18 and he was 34.

The ship the *Charlotte Jane* was built in Bristol for Thomson and Co by William Paterson. She was a wooden, three mast, 729 tonnage sailing ship sheathed in yellow metal, copper fastened panels and registered with Lloyds of London to carry 150 passengers and 35 crew. She was 131 feet 7 inches (40.1m) long, 35 feet 3 inches (10.9m) wide and 21 feet 7 inches (6.6m) deep.

The *Charlotte Jane* set sail on 2nd July 1848 carrying emigrants to Sydney Australia. The first few days were difficult with so many people being seasick as they encountered rough weather. Later Alexander described the traditional high jinks and water fights that took place when the ship crossed the equator. Miriam waxed lyrical describing the beauty of the sea, the sunsets and the wildlife. She also told of fierce storms.

After visiting friends in Australia, they were sent to Hong Kong carrying cows and horses. They encountered whirlwinds and narrowly escaped shipwreck. Sea charting in those days was not very accurate and extra vigilance was required to avoid rocks. From Hong Kong they sailed to Singapore. Miriam delighted in the glorious fruits but was warned to remain indoors when alone as there were many tigers on the island. They then sailed on to Bombay where they stayed for some weeks with friends while the ship had to have several of its metal panels refitted. Miriam was delighted with all the hustle and bustle of the city and enjoyed sight-seeing. They returned via Singapore and Hong Kong to Canton, (Whampoa) to load with tea to take back to England. Miriam mentioned the smell of onions and opium being overpowering. But we are not clear whether the *Charlotte Jane* was used to carry opium at some stage during the voyage.

On the way to Canton, in the South China Sea, Miriam gave birth to her second child, a boy called Alexander after his father. Whilst anchored for five months in Whampoa, the Captain and Miriam found life hard. It was difficult to go on shore, the tea was delayed and they were impatient to get home. Finally, they were able to set sail, stopping for a week in Table Bay, Cape Town, South Africa, arriving in London on 13th April 1850.

Miriam wrote her memoir in 1888, two years after her husband, Alexander died and 40 years after the voyage. The log book was written four times a day, every day during the voyage. I have combined the whole memoir with parts of the log book, the letters and my own comments. There is a lot in the log book that I could not read and also that I did not understand, but I hope what I have included gives a flavour of the voyage, and something of the character of Captain Alexander Lawrence. It has been necessary to alter his punctuation in some places, but I have decided to retain his ungrammatical use of "a.m/p.m and A.m/P.m, throughout.

Having spent so much time struggling to read each person's hand writing I have decided to choose a different font for each person. When widowed, Miriam looked back to write of a happier time, when she was a young woman of 20 with her beloved Alexander and her little baby, on her first voyage. Her letters were written at the time when she was actually 20. In order to differentiate between her 2 ages, I have selected a different font to that in the memoir.

Beside the memoir and log book, the information for this book has come mainly from family letters and journals and so may belong to well held family beliefs rather than verified facts! What I have written, is to the best of my knowledge correct.

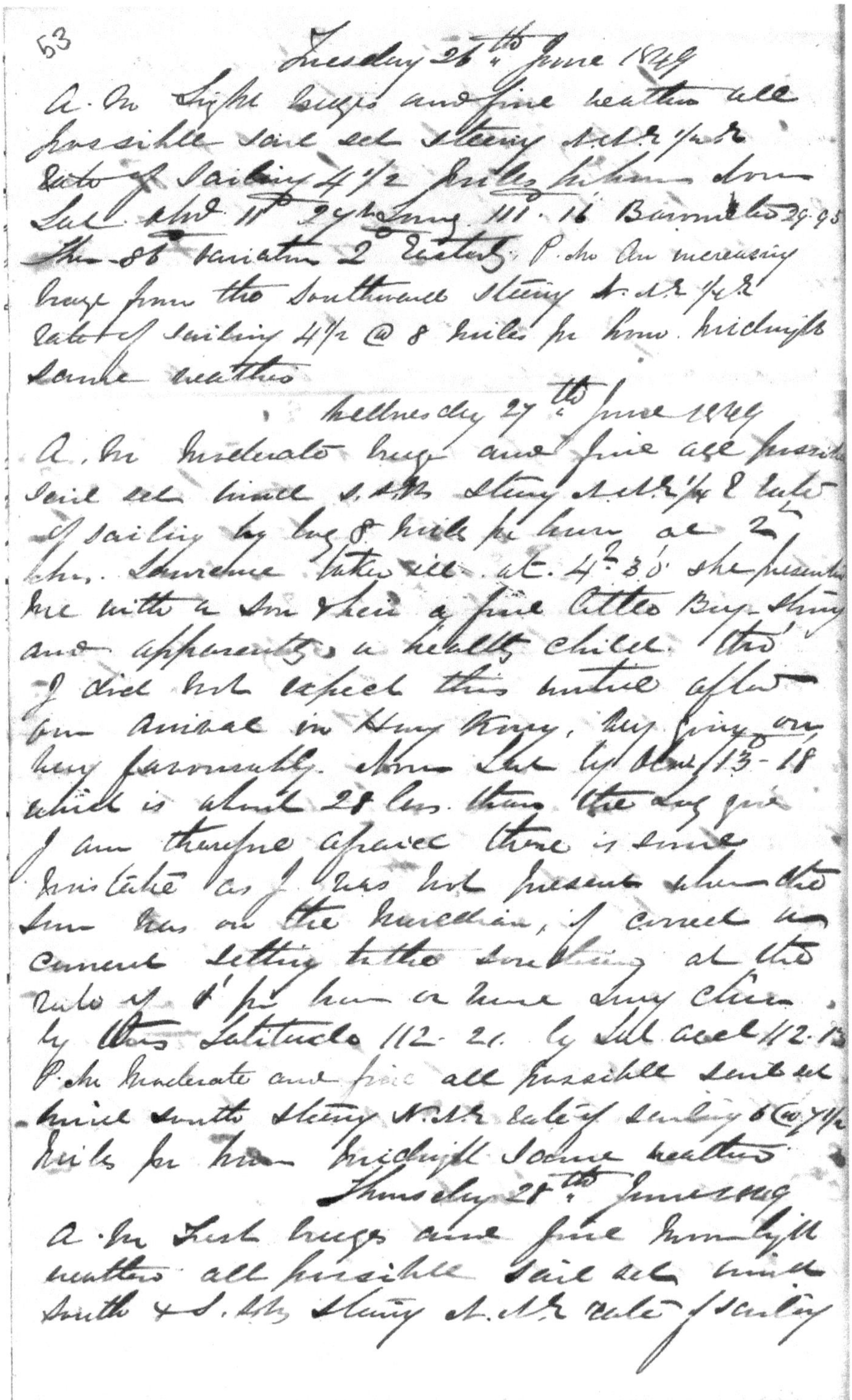

53

[Handwritten log book page — Alexander Lawrence's log]

Tuesday 26th June 1849

Wednesday 27th June 1849

Thursday 28th June 1849

A page from Alexander Lawrence's log book, for June 27th 1849, the day of the birth at sea of the Lawrence's son, Alexander Macclesfield Lawrence. (original size: 20 x 32 cm)

Central part of a letter written in 1848 by Miriam to her father from the *Charlotte Jane*.

Miriam and Alexander Lawrence in middle age (Alfred Charles Barker photograph from the Alfred Charles Barker collection, Canterbury Museum, Christchurch, New Zealand; image 1957.13.656)

Miriam Anne Lawrence when young.

Captain Alexander Lawrence when young.

Alexander Lawrence when old.

Dr Boddy, Miriam's father.

Miriam Lawrence with her youngest child William Stanley born 1871

Chapter 1

MIRIAM BODDY AND
ALEXANDER LAWRENCE

Miriam's memoir opens with a poignant paragraph about herself as a widow.

My life is done, the zest of my life is gone and I am alone. Such sorrows are contained in that one word only a widow knows. Musing quietly by my fireside my past life seems spread out before me like a large landscape on which are mapped out rivers of pleasures, forests of gloom and behind all mountains purpled and golden in the light of the setting sun, with crags and precipices softened by the blue mists of distance and only the highest points visible. Truly looking back, I can say, "Goodness and mercy have followed me all the days of my life."

I have thought a little account of my early married life when voyaging with my husband might prove amusing to my grandchildren. They may see the hand of providence in many things and wonderful preservation in the midst of many dangers by land and sea.

To begin then. My dear husband [Captain Alexander Lawrence] *was born in 1813 in Arbroath, it being then a small fishing village. He ran away to sea at the age of 12, persuading a cousin of his mother to take him as a boy. The vessel the Ariadne was small and in the Baltic trade, the hardest of all services. His sufferings were great but his pluck and determination carried him through and his harsh experiences at that time made him what he was, one of the cleverest seamen afloat. He gradually rose through the different grades and eventually at the age of 24, got command of the*

David Grant belonging to an uncle an East India merchant. A year or two afterwards through Mr Grant's influence he got command of the Lady Clark belonging to the firm of Thomson and Co now Anderson and Anderson. She was a ship of 500 tons then, 1838, considered a good size of vessel. She traded between London and Calcutta. The continual urbanity and kindness shown to the passengers and her quiet passages caused her to become a favourite passenger vessel. The Lady Clark and Captain Aleck Lawrence were well known names. She was always full.

ALEXANDER'S PARENTS AND SIBLINGS

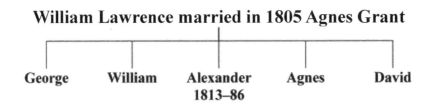

William Lawrence married in 1805 Agnes Grant

George   William   Alexander   Agnes   David
1813–86

Not much is known about Alexander's parents. His mother, Agnes Grant is said to have been very good looking and sweet tempered. She had a brother who was a city merchant and her sister married a Mr Menzies who was involved in growing sugar in Jamaica.

MIRIAM'S PARENTS AND SIBLINGS

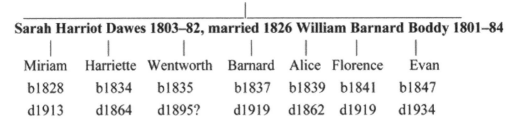

Sarah Harriot Dawes 1803–82, married 1826 William Barnard Boddy 1801–84

Miriam	Harriette	Wentworth	Barnard	Alice	Florence	Evan
b1828	b1834	b1835	b1837	b1839	b1841	b1847
d1913	d1864	d1895?	d1919	d1862	d1919	d1934

Miriam Anne Boddy was born on 18 June 1828. She was the eldest child of Sarah Harriot Boddy and William Barnard Boddy and was baptized on 10 October of that year at Newington St Mary in Surrey. As a young man Miriam's father, William and his three brothers had all been in the navy, however disaster struck the family. His mother went to greet two of her sons off their ship and was faced with the shattering news that both of them had been drowned at sea. Since a third brother had been wounded at sea and invalided out of the navy with a pension for life, William came out of the navy. He became a surgeon. As well as his private practice he was said to have been a medical officer to the Fishmonger Company and to a small hospital for old people.

From the few letters we possess which are written by him, he comes across as a kindly, upright and perhaps rather lugubrious person, much involved in his medical practice. He appears to have given advice and treatment to many of his friends and family and in a letter to Miriam he complained of the difficulty of getting them to pay him. Though irritated by this he appears to have been loath to pressure them too much for fear of causing lasting feuds and frictions.

Miriam's mother's letters portray her as being deeply religious and devoted to her children, though somewhat distracted and weighed down by them all! Both parents' letters refer to the noisiness of their boys who I believe were sent away to boarding school whilst the girls had lessons at home when little and then went to day school.

Nothing is known about Miriam as she grew up except that when writing her memoir, she remembered a geography book which she said had instilled in her a longing to travel. Photographs of her as a young woman show her as short, slender and attractive.

William and Sarah Boddy lived in Saville Row, Camberwell, London where they raised their large family

Miriam next wrote about how she and Alexander first met each other:

I first met the dear partner of my life on 1st January 1846. A curious circumstance is connected with this meeting. Daguerreotype portraits were just coming into fashion. Walking one afternoon in London, along Parliament Street, with a cousin, I saw in a window one or two Daguerreotypes of individuals, one of which I pointed out to my cousin as a nice looking, man. I thought no more of it till on that New Year's Day I saw the same portrait laying on my aunt's table. I asked who it was. She said, "it is my cousin

Alexander Lawrence. He commands the Lady Clark and he will very likely be here tonight. As she was speaking the gentleman himself walked in.

Our acquaintance soon became a sincere affection and on 25th February 1847 I became his wife.

It is curious how things go. One thing grows out of another. I always say I owed my husband to a broken leg! My father was a doctor and was called to see a child who had been run over and had her leg broken. My mother and her mother, Mrs Menzies, became very intimate. At her house my mother's brother met Mrs Menzies's cousin and actually married her. It was in their house that I first met my husband.

The marriage of Miriam and Alexander took place at St Peter's Church Walworth, in the parish of Camberwell, London. Soon afterwards the couple travelled to Scotland to meet some of Alexander's family. We have an interesting letter from Miriam's mother written to her newly married daughter.

6 Saville Row
Walworth
March 26th 1847

My dear Miriam

I received your kind letters with which I was much pleased and hasten to answer them, not the least doubting you will be glad to hear from home. In the first place we are all quite well and for myself my health is much better than when you left. As for baby he improves wonderfully, he endeavours to get on his feet so perhaps if you make your stay very long, in Scotland he will be able to walk to his christening. Trotty [one of Miriam's sisters] longs for your return indeed we shall all be pleased to see you when the time is fixed. Everyone is enquiring when you are expected. I tell them that is a question which cannot be answered. I suppose when inclination leads. That you were so well received did not at all surprise me though of course I feel much pleasure that you should meet with so much kindness so far from home and amongst strangers.

I hope and trust your life will always keep as smooth as it is at present but do not in the midst of all your enjoyment forget Him who is the giver of all good. Never fail to thank Him for all his mercies and I trust you always offer your morning prayers to him and likewise evening to thank Him for all His blessings through the day.

We were pleased that Mrs Steel [Alexander's sister] has family prayers. It makes one feel more comfortable to know you are with serious persons. Pray thank Mrs Steel from me for her very great kindness to you. I hope one day to be able to thank her in person.

[Everyone] is very pleased with Captain Lawrence. I have plenty of long salutations upon having become a mother- in-law. I hope my son will prove very dutiful to me. You enjoyed the ball very much I find but your resolution of not going to another gratified me. May you keep your resolve. It must have been an animating sight after all, for according to all account they dance in good earnest in Scotland. Suppose you joined.

The letter continues with a lot of family news which is not relevant here. It ends:

Your Papa sends his kind love to you both and will write soon, he unites with me in saying we long for your return suppose you will let us know when you propose to do so. My kind love to Maria and Jane Menzies when you see them and also to my son Alick and

Believe me

Your ever affectionate Parent

I am tired

S. H. Boddy

Miriam wrote:

On our return from our wedding my husband determined to pass as A 1 Commander, he being only 2nd class. How he worked overcoming all obstacles and they were many. Thanks to his pluck and perseverance he

5

passed A 1. During this time, we lived at Walworth Terrace. A more miserable time, I never spent my husband being entirely absorbed in his difficult studies. I saw nothing of him, besides which I was far from well. [Meaning she was pregnant.] *However, time passed. Thompson and Co were to build a new ship to trade to Australia and Alexander was to look after their interests while it was being built, so we were sent to Bristol in the July of 1847. She was to be the largest wooden vessel that had been built for that time, for the Merchant Service. As he faithfully did his duty, he got into hot water with the builder who was none other than William Patterson, the famous ship builder who worked with Isambard Kingdom Brunel on the ships the Great Britain and the Great Western.*

It is quite likely that they may have argued about the rigging of the ship. Alexander would have had no say with anything to do with the design of the hull but might have been allowed some influence upon the rigging. Master's often had specific opinions on such matters.

The ship was a wooden sailing ship. She was sheathed on her sides with metal panels, which I believe, were to prevent barnacles attaching themselves to the wood and gradually weighing the ship down, and to protect against wood burrowing worms.

Whilst Miriam awaited her baby, in Bristol, one of her sisters, Florence known as Trotty, went to stay with her and contracted measles. Fortunately, this occurred well after the first three months of Miriam's pregnancy. Miriam received a chatty letter from her mother.

6 Saville Row
Walworth
Nov 2nd 1847

My dear Miriam

At length I am able to spare 5 minutes to write to you no doubt you have expected to hear long before but you are quite aware how much my time is occupied particularly since the children have been ill. I am happy to say they are both quite recovered. They are looking thinner that is all.

Baby has not been taken off his feet he runs about everywhere foraging out all the mischief possible. I am very glad Trotty has got over the measles so well. I did not feel the least uneasy about her, being perfectly satisfied that she would be taken care of perhaps more so than if she had been at home. The only thing you have to take care of now is that she does not take cold, though I do not think there is much fear of that the weather being so very mild. I feel very dull sometimes, like a bird upon a housetop, particularly of an evening for Harriette [the eldest of Miriam's sisters] is no companion and your Papa either queer or out. When you write say if you can when you are likely to want me, for I have made up my mind to come to you if nothing happens to prevent me. Have you got everything in readiness.

I would have my nurse with me a little while before you want her you being quite a novice in these matters. Bye the bye how do you like your doctor does he seem a pleasant good-tempered man.

I find I have some few things of yours still such as two flannel jackets and drawers and socks, they shall come with me. Be sure Florence says her prayers. Does she like going to school. You must have been highly amused at Harriette's letter. Always tell her of her spelling whenever you write. She does not manage particularly well at Miss Eisdell's they think her a strange child and well they may.

I was surprised your father returned so soon from Bristol he should have stayed with you for he was very comfortable. He wished he had afterwards but he is like his daughter H rather an oddity. He is in much better health as for myself I am better than I have been for some month's past. Alice sends her love and she is quite lonely without Trotty. I assure you I miss her very much. You are to write to Harriette something she can answer, pray put some puzzling question for fun. Suppose you will have plenty of fireworks on Friday, we shall have none the Boys being away. They are quite well. Has Wenty [One of Miriam's brothers] written yet. Your Papa intends writing to

Alick tomorrow when he will tell him about Uncle George. I must hastily conclude having some time to get dressed. They all send their kind love and give plenty for Florence,

My love to Alick and yourself. Hoping soon to hear from you. Your ever Affectionate parent. S H BODDY.

There is no record of whether Miriam's mother came for the birth, which took place on 15th December 1847, or whether her nurse attended but it seems unlikely as Miriam wrote:

In Bristol my first dear little baby was given to me and I must here record the extreme kindness shown to me by Mrs Patterson [probably the wife of William Patterson the shipbuilder.] *A young girl of 19 I needed all the help I could get. My baby was not pretty but she was my own darling. She was very good and dearly did I love her. I liked to dress her in the pretty clothes I had made entirely myself. We christened her or rather Dr Hamilton did so, Harriet Agnes after my mother and sister-in-law Mrs Steel. The ship was at last finished and christened by the name of the wife of one of the owners the Charlotte Jane. Mrs Rigmaiden wife of an old true friend performed the ceremony. She was the largest ship that had been built in Bristol* [For the Merchant service].

The Bristol Mirror recorded the event.

"*The Charlotte Jane,* 17th April 1848 from Patterson's yard, Bristol. Precisely as the clock struck one, Mrs Rigmaiden of London, the sponsor of the ship, dashed a bottle of wine against her bow and having named her the *Charlotte Jane*, the dog-shore was knocked away and the noble vessel, which was gaily decorated with flags of every description, descended slowly and majestically into her native elements"

Miriam noted:

My Husband brought her to London.

No of Certificate 394.

Address of Bearer 1 Sutherland Street, Walworth Road Surrey

Date and Place of Birth 1813 Arbroath Forfar

No of Register Ticket New

Signature Alexander Lawrence

This Certificate is given in Exchange for a First Class certificate granted at London on the Thirtieth day of August 1847

Any person who fraudulently forges or alters a Certificate or fraudulently makes use of any Certificate to which he is not justly entitled is liable either to be prosecuted for a Misdemeanor or to be summarily punished before a Magistrate by a penalty of £50 or by imprisonment with hard labour for three months and any person who refuses to deliver up a Certificate which has been cancelled or suspended is liable to the same summary punishment

Issued at the PORT of London in the 18th day of Sept 1851

Certificate of A1 Competency as Master granted to Alexander Lawrence in August 1847, confirmed in September 1851 under the Mercantile Marine Act 1850

Model of the *Charlotte Jane* (courtesy the Canterbury Museum, Christchurch, New Zealand; image 384/50)

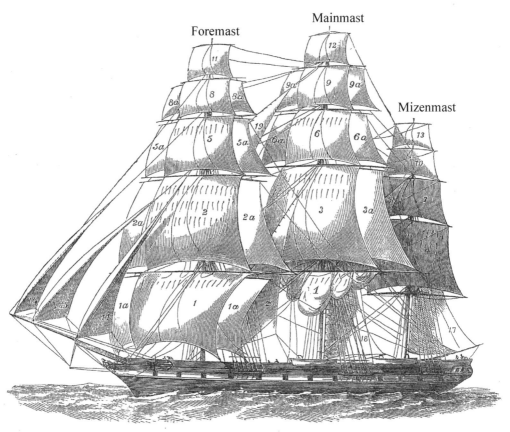

Foremast Mainmast Mizenmast

Fig. 4.

1, Course; 1a, Studding-sails; 2, Fore-topsail; 2a, Studding-sails; 3, Main-topsail; 3a, Studding-sails; 4, Mizen-topsail; 5, Fore-topgallant-sail; 5a, Studding-sails; 6, Main-topgallant-sail; 6a, Studding-sails; 7, Mizen-topgallant-sail; 8, Fore-royal-topsail; 8a, Studding-sails; 9, Main-royal-topsail; 9a, Studding-sails; 10, Mizen-royal-topsail; 11, Fore-skysail-topsail; 12, Main-skysail-topsail; 13, Mizen-skysail-topsail; 14, Fore-topmast-staysail jib; 15, Jib; 16, Flying jib; 17, Mizen spanker; 18, Spenser; 19, Main-royal-staysail; 20, Main-topmast-staysail; 21, Mizen-topgallant-staysail.

A square-rigged ship with the whole of her canvas shown; Figure 4 from 'Sail – Sailings' in Chambers Encyclopaedia Vol VIII, 1882

Definition from Chambers Encyclopaedia Vol VI, 1882, p359:- "MAST, an upright, or nearly upright spar, resting on the Keelson of a ship, and rising through the decks to a considerable height, for the purpose of sustaining the yards on which the sails are spread to the wind. It is usually in joints or lengths, one above the other, the lowest and strongest being the mast proper, distinguished by its position as the fore, main, or mizzenmast. Above this comes successively the top-mast, the top-gallant-mast, the royal-mast, and, though very rarely used, the sky-scraper.

Mizen is spelt with one 'z' in Vol V111 in Chambers Encyclopaedia and in Vol V1 with two. The log book spells it with one.

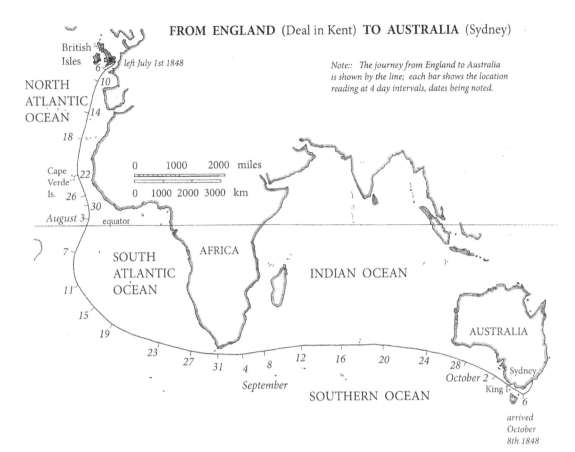

FROM ENGLAND (Deal in Kent) **TO AUSTRALIA** (Sydney)

British Isles
left July 1st 1848

NORTH ATLANTIC OCEAN

Cape Verde Is.

August 3 equator

SOUTH ATLANTIC OCEAN

AFRICA

Note:: The journey from England to Australia is shown by the line; each bar shows the location reading at 4 day intervals, dates being noted.

0   1000   2000   miles
0   1000 2000 3000   km

INDIAN OCEAN

AUSTRALIA

Sydney

September

SOUTHERN OCEAN

October 2

King I.

arrived October 8th 1848

The *Charlotte Jane*, sketched from a boat during sunset in the tropics by James Edward Fitzgerald during her 2nd voyage to New Zealand (courtesy the Canterbury Museum, Christchurch, NZ; image 1938.238.9)

Chapter 2

TO SYDNEY AUSTRALIA

100 days at sea

Thomson and Co decided that Alexander should sail the *Charlotte Jane* to Sydney, Australia carrying emigrants.

Miriam wrote:

After a great deal of consideration my husband consented that I should go with him on his first voyage on the Charlotte Jane. This to me, a young girl whose travels had been confined to a 30-mile journey in a stage coach, was like the opening of paradise.

Accordingly, in the month of August [2nd July 1848] *we sailed from the Downs* [anchorage near Deal.] *We were bound for Sydney. We took 300 or 400 emigrants and four passengers.*

The *Charlotte Jane* was in fact carrying 264 emigrants including the children. This is a far larger number than the 150-passenger capacity recorded in the Lloyd's register for the *Charlotte Jane*, and a much smaller number than Miriam's vague estimate of 300 or 400!

I have not been able to find a passenger list but I have found a document from the New South Wales Gazette that states that 264 Immigrants arrived in Port Jackson, Sydney on the *Charlotte Jane*, on 11th October 1848. It provides a record of their occupations.

Amongst the men there were 56 agricultural labourers, 6 gardeners, 11 shepherds, 6 carpenters, 1 groom, 2 masons, 2 brick makers, 1 fitter and turner, 2 bricklayers, 5 blacksmiths, 1 sawyer, 1 domestic servant, 4 coopers, 1 clerk and 1 maltster. Amongst the unmarried women there were 27 house servants, 4 nursemaids, 3 dressmakers, 1 dairymaid and 1 housemaid. There were 41 married women and 95 children.

The above deck passengers were Dr Jamieson, the ship's Superintendent Surgeon, Miriam Lawrence, baby Harriet Lawrence, aged 6½-months and her nurse, Helen Ken or Pen, whose surname is very difficult to decipher in the log book.

Alexander's first entry in the log was without any heading or title. He wrote:

Sunday 2nd July 1848

This day I commence my journal, at 5 a.m close-in with Dunnose, Isle of Wight. The pilot, Murray left the ship for which I paid 3 pounds sterling. 10.30 down below with the Emigrants and performed Divine Service

Services were carried out by the Superintendent Surgeon as there was not a Chaplin on board. In good weather they were held on deck and in bad weather down below in the hold.

Noon squally with rain. Made several tacks during the afternoon and stood out from the Needles. 9.0'clock p.m blowing hard with very heavy rain. Emigrants suffering a good deal from seasickness.

Monday 3rd July 1848

Bill of Portland bearing West. Noon blowing very hard. My wife very sick as well as Miss Pen [Helen] and many of the emigrants. Baby very good but she cried during the day.

Wednesday 5th July 1848

Emigrants very well but their place below very damp and not particularly clean. The carpenter repairs the female water-closet below, all the water-closets below have leaked and are not in good order. Minnie [Miriam] and the baby quite well, Helen much better. The Start light house distant 8 miles from which I take my departure and I hope for good at least for the voyage. Rate of sailing between 6½ and 4 miles per hour.

Friday 7th July 1848

Strong breezes Ship pitching a good deal. The ship the Barham and the Barque which has been in company is Hull down on the Lee quarter. [Hull down is when a ship is at such a distance that, from the convexity of the globe, only her masts and sails are to be seen.]

Saturday 8th July 1848

Exchanged longitude with the Brig Easor from Oporto out 12 days. Inspected the emigrants this morning found their place very dirty made them take their beds and bedplaces on deck and clean the place well out.

At 3 p.m tacked ship rate of sailing 4 miles per hour.

At 8 p.m breeze increasing. Ship pitching a good deal at more wind. Carried away [broke] *the fore topmast and fore and main top gall masts. Strong breeze with rain at times and heavy head sea. People employed clearing away the wreck.*

This would have been very testing for a newly forming crew getting used to a new ship. I imagine everyone was feeling very anxious and frightened at such difficulties occurring after only a few days at sea. The noise of masts crashing down must be terrifying, added to the pitching of the ship.

Sunday 9th July 1848

A.m strong breezes from the west.
At daylight took mizen topsail in and mizen to make her steer. The
carpenter employed making another topmast.
Noon. Strong breezes no observations for longitude or latitude.
Divine service performed twice today by the surgeon at which the
Emigrants mostly appeared attentive. Midnight strong breeze with a
heavy head sea.

Monday 10th July 1848

A.m strong breezes from the North, rate of sailing 6 miles an hour.
At daylight cleared away for getting the topmast on end.

At 9 fitted it. Set a main topmast stud sail. Not being able to get
around much having had my foot bruised by the topmast falling on it.
Did not get up till eight p.m an increasing breeze, rate of sailing 4 to
7 miles per hour. At 4 p.m sent the fore top sail yard up. And haul
the sail. Sent up the top gallant mast (shut).

I wonder how many of the crew may also have been hurt by this
accident.
Alexander did not record any. I like to think that if there had been any
serious injuries he would have commented. But perhaps this might have
been noted in the Surgeon's records instead.

Tuesday 11th July 1848.

A.m carpenter finishing the main topgallant mast. P.m Sent main
topgallant mast aloft sent up sail and main royal yard.

Miriam did not mention any of these disasters. I think her grandchildren
would have been interested in the drama of masts crashing down onto the
deck and bruising their grandfather's foot and imagining the stricken ship
out in the wild sea labouring against the elements. It seems likely that she

had just forgotten the early hazards of the voyage, which leads me to conclude that Miriam was not writing her memoir with the log book to hand, as if she had had it, I am sure she would have included such a frightening and dangerous event. I imagine, she like everyone else at the time would have been very frightened. Later in the memoir there are errors in the route of the voyage. Had she had the log book to refer to she would have been able to correct them. There are also inaccuracies about the dates of sailings and arrivals which would have been very easy to check. Of course, we do need to remember that she was writing 40 years after the event! I do wonder how she remembered as much as she did all these years later. I feel so fortunate that the log book and the memoir have eventually been united with us.

On 12th July Alexander wrote:

Emigrants all pretty well, mustered them on deck and had their place below well serviced out. Could not get their beds on deck owing to the late accident of carrying away the topmast. P.m the hands finishing the jib boom which was carried away when the top mast fell.

I suppose it was routine practise for ships to carry all the equipment necessary to mend such things as broken masts but even so it is impressive, that everything appears to have been put right quickly, calmly and efficiently.

On 14th July Alexander reported that all the emigrants were adhering well to the ship's rules. They had to be out of bed by seven o'clock. Breakfast was at eight and their living quarters below deck had to be cleaned out by eleven. Soap was given out on certain days for clothes washing. The log book has many references to cleaning out and fumigating the emigrant's quarters and of the stoves being lighted, and all this being regularly and thoroughly inspected to ensure the highest possible standards of hygiene at all times.

This would have been vital for the health of all especially with such a crowded ship. It is impressive to note that there were no deaths recorded on this voyage to Australia. The stoves were part of the fumigating process, as substances such as sulphuric acid and vinegar were added to the fuel, to purify stale and possibly infectious air in the emigrant's quarters. Perhaps the stoves were also used for the emigrants cooking. Food rations were provided from the ship's store which I believe the emigrants cooked themselves, having a rota of people on cooking duty. Their meals were taken below at a long table fixed to the floor, between the rows of bunks on either side of the ship. The space would have been very cramped.

Single men slept in bunks 6½ feet (2 metres) long and two feet (0.6 metre) wide, whilst married couples were provided with bunks 3½ feet (1.1m) wide. It is possible they had a curtain to hang up to give some privacy. I imagine the children were fitted in about the place! All possessions had to be stored with their owners.

It was often damp below and lacking in fresh air. We know they had some toilets and presumably there were some sort of arrangements for bathing. Washing clothes in salt water even with soap must be a nightmare, but at least there would often have been a breeze which would have helped the clothes to dry, though I understand that spray from the sea flying up onto the drying washing meant the clothes stiffened with salt. This would have been a great problem especially for baby clothes and underwear chaffing the skin. Both Miriam and Helen and many of the female emigrants would have been menstruating and so needed a good supply of cloths to absorb their blood and these would all have had to be washed and worn again month after month. They would have been held in place with a belt around the waist onto which the cloth would be attached. In order for the sanitary cloths not to be recognisable on the washing line they were sometimes put inside a cotton bag and then hung up to dry, this was also probably a way of any staining being kept hidden and perhaps it also kept away some of the salt too. Of course, salt is very good for killing germs and when diluted good for promoting healing, so it may have had its uses!

Some women might have used a type of tampon made with a sponge, encased in a silk or cotton bag with a string attached so it could be removed easily from the vagina. The sponges could be rinsed out and used again and again which must have saved on the amount of washing needed.

I wonder how many women could afford silk and imagine that cotton may have been used instead or just a sponge on its own with some kind of string fixed to it. Baby nappies would also have had to be washed regularly and drying must have been a problem when it was foul weather. However, rain water was regularly collected for drinking and would have been much more efficient and pleasant to use when available.

I think in hot weather a seawater shower was sometimes rigged up, for the passengers, with surrounding canvas curtains and some sort of sieve secured above so that buckets of sea water could be poured through onto the person beneath. This was probably very refreshing and cooling when in the tropics. Whether this was available to the emigrants in steerage is not certain, but I like to think that they possibly created such inventions for themselves. Though I imagine some of the women might have been loath to expose their naked bodies with such a lack of privacy.

They were reaching the tropics when Alexander wrote:

Thursday 20th July 1848

A.m fresh trade wind and fine moonlight all possible sail set steering S W rate of sailing 8 miles per hour. Daylight ship on larboard quarter. Exchanged colours with her she is French. A disturbance this morning amongst the emigrants, one of them yesterday made open the hospital and several articles stolen from thence, place cleared out of £. [Trade winds are easterly winds that occur in the tropics. They blow from North East in the Northern hemisphere and from South East in the Southern Hemisphere.]

Miriam wrote excitedly:

Everything being new the voyage was a constant delight to me. Those who plough the waters (they don't sail) in steamers have no idea of the real charm of a sea voyage. A fine day in the Trades, the vessel scarcely moving, the sea sparkling in the sunlight, all sails set the fresh breeze blowing steadily make it one of the most delightful experiences. Near the Azores were to be seen the pretty little Nautilus or Portuguese Man of War,

THE MAIDEN VOYAGE OF THE CHARLOTTE JANE 1848 – 50

like a tiny boat with a purple sail. Then would come a shoal of dolphins, then a shoal of porpoises leaping and gambolling about the ship, which the sailors say is a sign of a storm. Then came flying fish, which by the way are the most delicious eating.

Apparently, there are many different types of flying fish. They have forked tails which they beat vigorously as they rise to the surface of the sea to propel themselves out of the water. As they take off out of the water, they spread out their pectoral fins to act as wings, which apparently must remain wet to enable the fish to flit out of the water. Once the fins become dry and stiff the fish fall back onto the water. When kept wet by the sea spray, they can rise quite high and sometimes even land on a ship's deck.

Wednesday 2nd August 1848

At 8 a.m had a complaint made by the surgeon that the hospital had been broken into and that about 8 lbs of sugar, a quantity of raisins, nearly a bottle of wine, and a little rum had been stolen. At 11 mustered the people aft, selected seven from amongst the most respected as jury men and heard the evidence of several, from which the jury found Alfred Baldwin, Alfred Collins, Jonathan Rickard, George Lushman, George Pain, and George Arkell guilty of having received the goods knowing them to have been stolen. Pain confesses to having divided the sugar amongst some of them but will not say whom. Pain and Collins, I think are the guilty parties of having entered the store room.

Whether the jury decided on a punishment or if the Captain did is not clear. Certainly, everyone would have been more on the lookout for such behaviours and the gossip flying around rife. Alexander seems to have known enough about the emigrants to be able to know who were the most respected and who were the more suspect.

On August 4th 1848 the ship crossed the equator. This is known as 'crossing the line' and was traditionally a great time for celebrating and horseplay.

Saturday August 5th 1848

At 10 a.m the seamen commenced going through the old custom, of shaving those of the crew who have not crossed the line before. Some of the emigrants joined in at their desire and most of them both men and women appeared to enjoy the throwing of water at each other and soused each other most effectively. Nor was it confined to the main decks for the mates and some of the female servants commenced on the poop [upper most deck] *and I believe Mrs L, myself and Miss Pen* [Helen] *were the only ones that escaped. All took it in good part and enjoyed it but N. Murry who appeared in high dudgeon about it and threatened to sue N. Stewart,* [the Chief Officer] *when he gets to Sydney. Noon. All over. Gave the crew and emigrants a glass of rum each for which they appeared very grateful.*

Miriam did not mention any of these excitements, so we have no way of knowing what she thought about them. I think it is possible that she may have hated the whole event and been very relieved to have 'escaped' as Alexander wrote. I imagine she was quite happy to watch but wonder if perhaps Helen might have been disappointed not to have been able to lark about with everyone else. It is not clear where Harriet was at this event as she is not mentioned, so perhaps Helen was expected to look after her and so could not join in.

I think the grandchildren would have enjoyed hearing about such pranks and horseplay. Alexander must have seen all these excitements many times over. We learnt from the diary of a passenger on Alexander's next voyage that he had joined in with great gusto and was described as having shinned up the rigging whilst being chased!

Monday 7th August 1848

A.m strong breeze and squally all plain sail set. P.m rate of sailing 9 miles per hour. Distance made good 209 miles.

I imagine Alexander was delighted with such a distance.

Thursday 10th August 1848.

Emigrants place well cleaned out and fumigated. People generally well several children rather weakly and one woman during last night had a miscarriage but is doing well.

Not much is known about individual emigrants. Some would have been going out to Australia to work for their bosses who would have travelled out ahead to set up some kind of livelihood and were then sending for their employees. Others may have been going out to start a new life and would be hoping to find work when they arrived. I managed to find out from the Internet http://www.mkheritage.co.uk/ghg/people/Hornerntro.html some information about William Horner who is said to have travelled on the *Charlotte Jane* in 1848 to Sydney, Australia. He was born about 1785 but apparently declared his age to be some 10 years younger to ensure his passage! He was apparently a widower, a brick maker and illiterate. He was travelling with two of his daughters, Mary Anne Horner aged 19 who could read and was a house servant and Ellen Horner who could also read and was 11 years old. Several other members of the Horner family were travelling to Sydney in 1848 on a different ship called the *Fairlie*.

Almost every day Alexander recorded that the emigrants' places had been cleaned out, fumigated or swept and were in good order. He was clearly very aware of the importance of this.

Friday 11th August 1848

Emigrants requested to see the Act of Parliament being unsatisfied with their rating which has been fully served out.

I think this may refer to the amount of food that is served out to each person. Keeping rules and regulations understood and adhered to will have been important in order to keep the emigrants from getting angry or riotous.

Sunday 13th August 1848

9 a.m emigrants all clean their places. Swept out and at 10.30 attended divine service and the crew tho' some were reluctant. After service called them all together and gave them a lecture.

He clearly expected his crew to attend services and carry out every order to the letter.

Monday August 14ᵗʰ 1848

I find from several and repeated applications during the voyage that the emigrants prefer a substitute for salt provisions for their children and the same occurred on the last two voyages with Emigrants, and I also find from the three voyages experience that one and all would rather have salt meat than soup and Bouillon for a great many either will not or, cannot eat it but throw it overboard.

It is difficult to be sure what exactly is meant in this passage but it shows Alexander's interest in the preferences of the emigrants and their concerns for their children. It would be distressing to watch people and children refusing to eat the ship's food and actually throwing it overboard. What exactly the emigrants' diet consisted of is not made clear in the log book, though the usual meals on board ship at that time were salt pork, salt beef, dried beans and peas, ships biscuits, porridge and any other dried foods available. Apparently, weevils were always a problem in the kitchens and maggot racing a popular pastime! Food would often become an obsessive form of conversation with moans and grumbles about the boring and repetitive meals and especially when the ship was heaving and rolling so that cooking on hot stoves became impossible.

Sometimes there would be a cow on board to provide milk if only for the children or perhaps only for the grand passengers. Poultry and other animals were also kept to provide eggs and fresh meat but perhaps this was not often given to the emigrants? I suspect that they may have been regularly dissatisfied with the food supplied and often left hungry.

Catering for such numbers must have been very complicated when the length of a voyage was not certain and food so perishable without the luxury of freezers and preservatives. Catching fish to eat when possible would have been such a delicious boost to the menu. Keeping adequate supplies of fresh water required meticulous planning and rainwater a wonderful luxury when plentiful. I have heard that those at sea sometimes experienced haunting dreams about fresh drinking water, which I gather often tasted of tar from the barrels in which it was stored. Ships sometimes had to break their voyages in order to replenish their dwindling supplies of food and water.

The log book continued.

Thursday 17th August 1848

Wind to south and very heavy rain. Getting as much rainwater as possible.

Friday 18th August 1848

The female Ferguson very low and lightheaded. The surgeon entertains very little hope for her recovery, conversed with her a little. She appears to have a strong and firm hope of falling asleep in Jesus and expressed a desire to have the Holy Sacrament administered but I scarcely feel myself qualified in administering so solemn a ceremony.

Saturday 19th August 1848

This morning the Ship cleaned fore and aft with ----- and Holystone [a sand stone for scrubbing decks] *and the Emigrants place well cleaned out. The female Ferguson more cheerful and altogether better, at her request the surgeon administered, the Holy Sacraments to her and several of the others received it at the same time.*

Sunday 20th August 1848

Performed Divine Service down below as the weather was very unsettled and squally.

Monday 21st August 1848

The surgeon has been laid up with a bilious attack. At 6 p.m one of the emigrants fell down from the ladder in the after hold and dislocated his shoulder.

Wednesday 23rd August 1848

Light Breeze. The woman Ferguson not so well. Surgeon better. Shot two Albatross. One, caught with a worsted thread, [and] a cape pigeon. Gave them to one of the emigrants for stuffing.

Presumably some kind of trap was made with a woollen thread which the bird failed to see and became entangled.

P.m had a complaint from N. Stewart, the chief officer about the man Roberts he was refractory and would not do his duty. Find that he refused to go out on the sheetline, for which he was sent to the top gal and royal masts which I do not approve of for it was wrong in asking him to go out on the bow end.

This is something that must regularly have taken place when an officer made a decision in the absence of the Captain but with which the Captain disagreed. I wonder what discussions took place after this but sadly we do not know anything further.

Thursday 24th August 1848

Lowered the boat down for the purpose of exercising. Shot an albatross and three cape pigeon. Rate of sailing 2½ miles per hour.

Saturday 26th August 1848

Rate of sailing 8½ miles per hour. The female Ferguson rather better and the other invalids better, place cleaned out. The decks and ship thoroughly cleaned.

Friday 1st September 1848

P.m rate of sailing 8½-9 miles per hour.

Saturday 3rd September 1848

A.m a very heavy sea. People more or less sick and some a little alarmed. P.m breeze increasing a very heavy cross sea evidently hindered from a current.

Monday 4th September 1848

People pretty well below. The female Ferguson the only one who was considered in a dangerous state is better.

Thursday 7th September 1848

Daylight. Almost calm. At 8 an increasing breeze and squally with showers.

Tuesday 12th September 1848

A.m strong gales with violent hail. Rate of sailing 10 miles per hour.

Miriam described the delights of sailing:

As we went further south numbers of beautiful Albatross, Cape Pigeons and Molly Hawks were to be seen incessantly keeping up their graceful wheeling flight, looking so graceful. There were likewise multitudes of Petrel.

In the Tropics there were the long calms accompanied by deluges of rain. The splendid sunrises and sunsets were simply gorgeous. The vessel under the influence of the long rolling waves would roll over and over, till she nearly dipped her yard arms in the water and then would slowly roll over as far onto the other side, every mast and plank groaning and creaking and the blocks going down with a banging clank, all the while the blazing sun making the sea look like molten gold. Many a time I watched the sun rise in the Tropics. First just a cool air would breathe across the water which I knew was the signal of the sun rising, then the faintest light would creep up on the horizon and opal mists spread around, then one or two crimson cloudlets would arise followed by another, then some lines of gold would appear on the horizon and the gorgeous pageant went on increasing in splendour till all was lost in the brilliant day.

About the Cape and Southern Hemisphere, we experienced a heavy gale and I was taken on deck to see it. How awfully green the waves were coming on like green dragons with white crests and threatening to engulf us. Just as they appeared to be on the point of swallowing us, we would find ourselves on the top of one looking down into a vast green gulf. It was all very beautiful and I had no fear then. Some storms there were but what did I care. My husband was the captain and I had perfect faith in his skill.

Miriam sounds so thrilled and delighted by the sea and had certainly got her sea legs!

Thursday 21st September 1848

A.m stormy gales. At 4 a.m gales with violent hail. Noon very hard gales with thick snow and hail squalls. Hatches closed except the aft one. People below suffering a great deal.

Saturday 23rd September 1848

A row between 2 of the emigrants, had [them] *brought aft on the quarter deck.*

I wonder if Miriam and Helen had rows. When I first read Miriam's memoir, I pictured Harriet's nurse as a middle-aged woman with great experience in looking after children, so I was surprised to find she was a young girl in her teens. What an amazing adventure for her to have embarked upon and what stories she may have had to tell to her children and grandchildren in later years!

I wonder how Alexander and Miriam coped with their differences and moods. However much they may have been in love, they were extremely reliant on each other and still adapting to being married and first-time parents. Although Alexander had many years of experience at sea, he had never taken a wife and baby with him on board ship before. Miriam was only 20 years old, a first-time mother and completely new to life at sea. Although Helen was there to help with the childcare Miriam would have also held responsibility for her wellbeing. For both girls it will have been an extraordinary change to find themselves living in such close proximity, day in and day out, with so many men. On parts of the voyage, they were the only females on board ship. They probably missed their friends and family greatly. Everything must have been so new and strange and it may have been very difficult to adapt to such a life, especially if you suffered from seasickness.

Miriam does not mention any of the emigrants personally, but I guess she would have been interested in them and enjoyed seeing them on deck, talking with them and hearing about their families and experiences. Later in the memoir she expressed regret when there were no passengers on board, as she found it less interesting. I expect she may have socialised with Dr Jamieson and the officers, particularly at meal times, but would have always had to be aware of the boundaries of rank and propriety. I do wonder how many times Helen may have fallen in love, being surrounded as she was by so many men! Some emigrants were employed to do washing, cleaning, and kitchen work for the captain, officers and passengers. So, Helen may have had opportunities to make friends and gossip with some of them. Miriam's social life would have been more formalised as she needed to uphold her status as the Captain's wife.

For most of the time from September 21st until October 3 the log book recorded gales, strong gales, squally showers and even thunder and lightning.

Sunday 24th September 1848

Noon. Barometer 29.60 and falling. Weather looking very unsettled. At 7 p.m heavy squalls with hail and snow. Midnight strong gales

Seamen and sailors lived dangerous and demanding lives especially at night in times of bad weather and rough seas, when they had to be up together in the icy rigging furling and reefing huge freezing sails, while the ship was rolling and plunging and the wind howling round.

Tuesday 26th September 1848

Mrs Gibson safely delivered of a fine boy.

Wednesday 27th September 1848

2 A.m sudden gale of wind. Rate of sailing $6\frac{1}{2}$ to $9\frac{1}{2}$ miles per hour.

Saturday 30th September 1848

Shipped a sea on the larboard [left] *beam which carried away a part of the bulwarks and a good deal went down in the emigrants' place.* [Bulwarks are the wood panelling surrounding a vessel above deck.]

How ghastly for the emigrants to have their quarters flooded. With continuing bad weather, the chance of drying out would have been very slim.

On 3rd October land was sighted, as they were nearing Australia, supposed to be Cape Cataney, but it appeared that they were not sure exactly where they were, which was worrying as there were reefs about that could seriously damage the ship. There are many instances when Alexander commented that he believed the sea charts to be inaccurate. Having sighted land, he recorded that he was;

keeping a hand on the fore yard and two hands on the forecastle as well as myself and mate looking out for Kings Island and the Harlequin reefs. Nothing in sight but the water perfectly smooth which makes me conclude that we are inside of the Kings Island

Thursday 5th October 1848

A.m light wind off the land.

Seeing land for the first time after a long voyage must have been a thrilling experience with everyone jostling to get a sighting. I gather people say they can smell the land!

Saturday 7th October 1848

A.m rate of sailing 9 miles per hour, at daylight made all possible sail, at 8.30 passed and changed colours with an American Barque whaling, at 10.30 passed two others. Noon. No land in sight. At 6 p.m the land at Jervis Bay bearing west, altered course to North. Midnight shortened sail.

On 8th October the *Charlotte Jane* arrived outside Sydney harbour and a pilot was taken on board to take her up into Port Jackson. Miriam wrote:

The harbour is incomparably beautiful. It was early morning. None of my experiences has equalled that arrival for exquisite pleasure. The glorious sunrise, the exhilarating air, the clearness of the atmosphere and the lovely scenery, as we proceeded up the harbour intoxicated me. All along we were continually coming upon little bays with silver sands and grottoes down which trickled silvery streams overhung by ferns and foliage. Then came the delight of anchoring. Only those who have been on a long voyage can understand the delight of hearing the thundering noise of the dropping of the anchor. Then the feeling of perfect quiet and security is delicious.

The night of our arrival in Sydney was wrecked by a very unpleasant occurrence. Some of the emigrants were offended at something. I do not know the cause and became very unruly, running about with knives and threatening all kinds of things, at which I was very alarmed. The alarm bell was set ringing and the Police made their appearance and took the ring leaders away.

This was not mentioned in the log book. Alexander recorded:

Sunday 8th October 1848

A.m let go the anchor at the mouth of Sydney Cove. Let the sails come down instead of furling them. This ends the voyage or passage.

So, it is not known what that fracas was about. Perhaps it involved the dreary N. Murry who threatened to sue N. Stewart during the crossing of the line celebrations! Miriam's description sounds as if there were several people involved and it was serious enough for the police to be called. But as it is not recorded in the log book one wonders whether Miriam's memory is incorrect, although it is perhaps possible that as the ship had reached its destination the log book was no longer in use.

What a very momentous moment arriving in Sydney would have been for the emigrants as they saw for the first time the land where their future lives would be lived.

In a supplement to the New South Wales Government Gazette dated Wednesday 11th October 1848 there is an announcement recording the arrival of the *Charlotte Jane* with 264 Immigrants on the eighth of October 1848 in Port Jackson and detailing the arrangements for the hiring of workers from the ship. [See notice Page 32.]

We also found a newspaper cutting reporting the goods that were exported from England into Sydney on the *Charlotte Jane.* It seems amazing that she was able to carry anything else as she already had more emigrants than allowed!

The Sydney Morning Herald. N.S.W.

Tuesday 11th October 1848 Page 2. IMPORTS.

9th October The *'Charlotte Jane'* Ship 729 tons. Captain Lawrence, from London; 200 tons common salt, 30 tons rock salt, 9 Hogsheads bath bricks, 25 deals, 10 cartels currants, 44 casks whiting, 2 crates blocks, 500 fire bricks, Mackintosh and Hirst: 100 kegs painters colours, Captain Lawrence: 176 packages window sashes, 2 crates venetian blinds, 16 boxes window glass, George Thorne and Co. 1 butt, 1 pipe, and 2 hogsheads wine, Campbell and Co: 2 hogsheads and 4 quarter casks Madeira wine: E.W. Layton and Co; 1 case, Sir A. Fitzroy; 21 cases and 5 bales merchandise, Smith and Croft: 12 cases, and 4 bales, Order.

No. 116.

SUPPLEMENT

TO THE

NEW SOUTH WALES

GOVERNMENT GAZETTE,

OF TUESDAY, OCTOBER 10, 1848.

Published by Authority.

WEDNESDAY, OCTOBER 11, 1848.

Colonial Secretary's Office,
Sydney, 11th October, 1848.

IMMIGRANTS PER " CHARLOTTE JANE."

HIS Excellency the Governor has directed it to be notified, for general information, that the Ship " Charlotte Jane," with 264 Immigrants, arrived on the 8th instant, in Port Jackson.

The callings of the adult Immigrants, and the number of each calling, are as follows, viz.:—

MALES.

	MARRIED.	SINGLE.
Agricultural Laborers...	22	34
Gardeners	1	5
Shepherds	5	6
Carpenters	2	4
Grooms	1	
Masons	1	1
Brickmakers	1	1
Fitters and Turners....	1	
Bricklayers..........	2	
Blacksmiths	4	1

MALES, Continued.

	MARRIED.	SINGLE.
Sawyers............	1	
Domestic Servants		1
Coopers		1
Clerks.............		1
Malsters		1

FEMALES. (UNMARRIED.)

House Servants	27
Nursemaids..........	4
Dressmakers	3
Dairy Maids	1
Housemaids	1

1st page of supplement to the New South Wales Government Gazette, October 11 1848

On Thursday, the Twelfth instant, persons desiring to obtain servants from this ship, will be admitted on board between the hours of 10, a. m., and 4, p. m.

Most of the unmarried females by this ship being members of families which have been forwarded by the Government into the Interior, the number left on board does not exceed twelve. The hiring of the male Immigrants will therefore be proceeded with on the same day.

Before 10 o'clock on the morning of Thursday, the Twelfth instant, or at any other times than those fixed, as above stated, for the hiring of the Immigrants, no stranger or person in quest of servants will be admitted, or allowed to remain on board. Strict orders have been given to the Policeman on duty in the Ship, to enforce the observance of this rule.

All applications for servants must be made to the Surgeon Superintendent on board, and the Immigrants will be cautioned against hiring themselves to any person without his sanction, and without a formal agreement, to be signed by the two contracting parties, and witnessed by an Officer of the Immigration Department, who will attend on board of the ship for the purpose.

Before sanctioning any engagement, the Surgeon Superintendent will be required to satisfy himself of the respectability of the hiring party, either by reference to the Officer of the Immigration Department who will be in attendance, or by such other means of enquiry as may be available. This rule will be observed in every instance, but it will be acted upon with especial strictness in the case of the unmarried females ; and these latter will be recommended not to accept situations in Inns or other Houses of public entertainment, as it is considered that such places are better suited to servants who have been for some time in the Colony, than to Immigrant girls on their first arrival.

No stranger will be allowed to visit the 'tween decks of the vessel unless accompanied by the Surgeon Superintendent. Any person infringing this rule will be ordered to quit the ship forthwith.

The Ship will be anchored at the entrance of Sydney Cove, and will be provided with an external accommodation ladder.

By His Excellency's Command,
E. DEAS THOMSON.

Colonial Secretary's Office,
Sydney, 11th October, 1848.

2nd page of supplement to the New South Wales Government Gazette, October 11 1848

The Surgeon would have had a busy day overseeing all the arrangements for the hiring of the immigrants off the ship, whilst for them it must have been unnerving waiting to see who was interested in hiring them and wondering whether things would work out well. It is not clear whether any immigrants did not get offered a position, and if so, what happened to them.

How exciting for Miriam and Helen to have arrived at last and what a relief to be safely on land once again. Little Harriet must have been very amazed at the new world around her. Walking on firm land would have felt very strange for a little while, after the constant motion of the ship.

Miriam reminisced:

While in Sydney we experienced much kindness and hospitality. One pleasant excursion stands out in my memory. It was an oyster procure. A party of us sailed away to an oyster bed each carrying a hammer. On board there was a hamper filled with all good things. The amusement was for each to knock his own oysters for himself off the rocks and after all had collected sufficient, to consume them in company with the usual accompaniments. I cannot say I broke off many but I remember I got plenty to eat. The sail home in the moonlight through a sea brilliant with phosphorous light was most enjoyable.

We received an invitation to visit the Menzies, a cousin of my husband living on the banks of the Minnamurra river in the beautiful district of Illawarra. We started one morning in a miserable little steamer when Helen and I were regrettably miserably sick. The steward kept ordering us to, "Shift yourself, you will be much better if you shift yourself." Glad were we when we got to Wollongong, the sea port where we were met by Mr Menzies who drove us to his home. [Presumably in some sort of horse drawn carriage.]

On our way we passed through a splendid forest of old gum trees where were large flocks of black cockatoos with yellow crests and numbers of little green parrots, which appeared as plentiful and impudent as our sparrows. The yellow crested cockatoos are now, they say, very rare. We forded a deep river then on again over very rough roads. The air is fresh and balmy, full of spicy forest scents with the exhilarating feel of perfect purity. After several hours we took a rest in a miserable shanty at a roadside inn to eat a few biscuits. There seemed to be no provisions in this primitive place. It was pretty late at night when we arrived at our destination. We remained with Mrs Menzies almost a week amusing ourselves with wandering about. We were taken to see the family cemetery where there was a small grave of an infant of our hosts on a hill surrounded by trees looking so lonely. We went one day some miles away over 'corduroy roads' to visit a family who had been among the first emigrants. They were pleased to see women from the old country and gave us cowslip wine and homemade cake looking wistfully at us when we said we were going back. The young women were dressed in the fashion of some years back and looked very quaint.

I met with a funny adventure one afternoon. I was wandering alone on the banks of the river watching the gambols of some duckbilled platypus, a kind of otter, when suddenly without noise or warning I found myself surrounded by a large number of natives in native costume, that is to say a blanket fastened round the neck and carrying a bundle of spears in one hand. I was very frightened but soon found they were not attending to me but were running on swiftly and softly. In a moment they disappeared behind the trees as suddenly and silently as they had come. I lost no time in betaking myself indoors but I was told there was no need for alarm, Mr Menzies being kind to them they were harmless. But to see, coming from you did not know where, 50 savages hideously ugly and close to you, was very alarming to me.

I was very sorry to leave the pretty place and my kind hostess.

Her kind hostess was Margaret Menzies who had four daughters and a son all under the age of eight. Harriet will have had a wonderful time being carried about and mothered by the girls and interested in Archibald who was aged two. Miriam would have revelled at being in a lively family household with Margaret to chat with about babies, parenting, news from mutual friends and family, and living in Australia. Robert and Margaret had gone out to Wollongong in 1839 and having bought land built themselves a house. They planned to make their fortune and eventually return home to Scotland.

Miriam and Alexander remained in Australia for about five weeks and when not on shore they would have stayed onboard the *Charlotte Jane*. We have a rather fraught letter that Miriam wrote to her mother right at the end of their stay.

Ship Charlotte Jane
Sydney

November 1848

My dear Mama,

I just write to tell you that we are just about leaving Sydney for China where we hope to arrive in about 6 weeks or 2 months, since we are in the stream waiting till a fair wind comes and I dare say we shall start tomorrow. Alick and I and Ellen [interestingly both log book and memoir refer to her as Helen, though in all the letters she is called Ellen] are quite well but the baby is not quite the thing. I think her teeth are annoying her she has only got 2 yet. The other day she was very poorly and we had to send for a doctor, our doctor who goes with us being out.

I have enjoyed my stay on shore very much. I had a trip to Illawarra, the country there is very pretty and Mr Robert Menzies has a very nice place indeed.]

Why have you not written? I have longed for a letter by every ship and there have been two or three since we have been here. It surely could not have been much trouble to write a few lines and send them. I should very much like to hear how you are getting on and now I can't hear from you till I get back. I don't know how long we shall stay in China perhaps three months which is not very pleasant to look forward to. It seems there is no society except at Hong Kong and I don't think we shall go there.

The people here in Sydney have made themselves very agreeable indeed they all seem pleasant people. We have no passengers and

I am afraid I shall find it rather dull. We are taking some cows and some very nice horses. I have no time to say anymore as Alick is going ashore and waits this letter.

Give my fondest love to Papa and my little brothers and sisters and to all enquiring friends and accept the same yourself in which Alick joins.

From your truly affectionate daughter,

Minnie A. Lawrence

Ellen sends her love to you all and is in great fright for fear of her being sick.

Poor Miriam she does sound low. It must have been very disappointing not to have heard from home and she sounds as if she was dreading the next part of the journey with no passengers and only cows and horses for company. Perhaps she and Ellen were fearful about going through the agony of being seasick all over again. Especially as Miriam by this time was pregnant, perhaps feeling queasy and unwell, and worried about where the next baby would be born and quite simply, longing for home.

However, forty years later Miriam painted a different picture in the memoir.

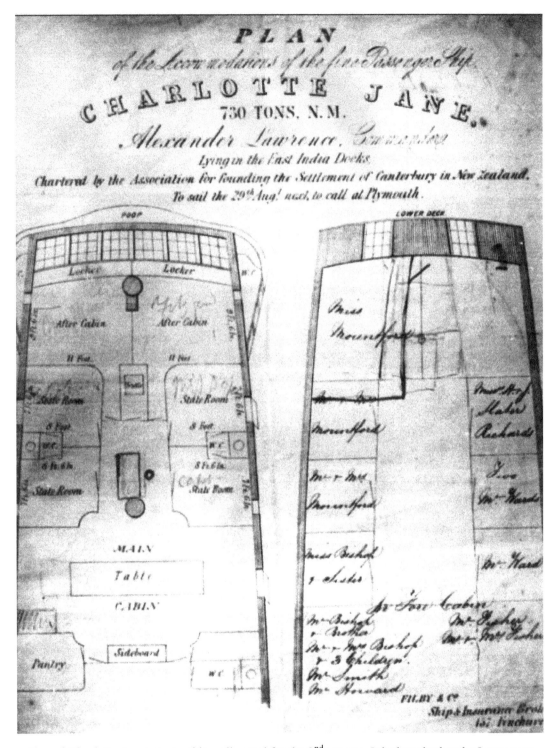

Plan of *Charlotte Jane's* stern cabins, allocated for the 2nd voyage. It is thought that the Lawrences occupied the right 'poop' after cabin, the doctor the left 'poop' after cabin and Helen a right hand state room. '(Canterbury Pilgrims & Early Settlers Association Inc collection, Canterbury Museum, NZ; image 1949.148.216)'

Photographs from above of the stern and bow ends of the Canterbury Museum model of the
Charlotte Jane. (photo by Phyl Thorpe)

Probably the *Charlotte Jane* as depicted on "Sailing Ships-the voyage out" (courtesy teara.govt.nz)

Deck of the *Charlotte Jane* at sea from the starboard quarter boat, ink drawing be Alfred Charles Barker.
(Canterbury Museum, Christchurch, New Zealand; image 19XX.2.183)

Sailors furling a sail at sea, photograph by Alan Villiers (copyright National Maritime Museum, Greenwich, London; image N61499)

After poop deck cabin of the *Charlotte Jane* from the 1850 watercolour by James Edward Fitzgerald, 1818-1896. (Canterbury Pilgrims & Early Settlers Association Inc collection, Canterbury Museum, NZ; image 1949.148.307)

EC181.60

Chest of shallow drawers used for medicines and instruments by the doctor on the *Charlotte Jane*. This chest was brought to New Zealand on board the *Charlotte Jane* in 1850 by Dr Alfred Charles Barker. (Barker collection, Canterbury Museum, Christchurch, New Zealand; image EC181.60)

Campbell's Wharf, Sydney Cove, from a print circa 1842 (author's collection)

View of Darling Harbour, Sydney, circa 1850 (courtesy Mitchell Library, State Library of New South Wales; image no. 431583)

SYDNEY TO HONG KONG AND ON TO SINGAPORE

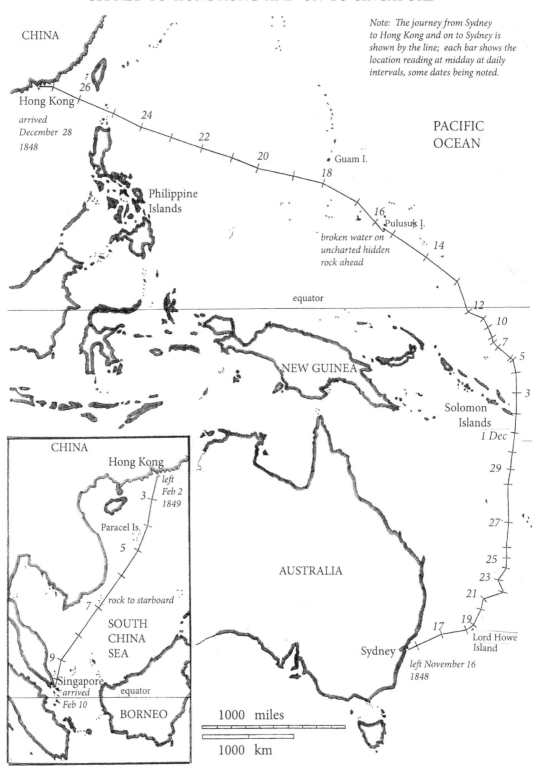

Note: The journey from Sydney
to Hong Kong and on to Sydney is
shown by the line; each bar shows the
location reading at midday at daily
intervals, some dates being noted.

CHINA

PACIFIC
OCEAN

26

Hong Kong

*arrived
December 28
1848*

24

22

20

18

Guam I.

Philippine
Islands

16

Pulusuk I.

*broken water on
uncharted hidden
rock ahead*

14

equator

12

10

7

5

3

NEW GUINEA

Solomon
Islands

1 Dec

29

27

25

23

21

CHINA

Hong Kong

*left
Feb 2
1849*

3

Paracel Is.

5

AUSTRALIA

19

17

Lord Howe
Island

Sydney

*left November 16
1848*

7

rock to starboard

SOUTH
CHINA
SEA

9

Singapore
*arrived
Feb 10*

equator

BORNEO

1000   miles

1000   km

44

Chapter 3

SYDNEY TO HONG KONG
43 days at sea

AND ON TO SINGAPORE
9 days at sea

Miriam wrote with much enthusiasm:

It was decided that we should go from Sydney to China, Hong Kong instead of home. Great was my delight at this news. To think I was to go to that most wonderful country. In those days China was a mystery land and very little known to anyone as they were very jealous of foreigners. Very few ladies had been to the celestial land. From my earliest years I had longed to go having read a great deal about it in an old Goldsmith's geography.

The log book recorded that the *Charlotte Jane* left Sydney on

Wednesday 15th November 1848

Came on board and found that the men which were shipped in Sydney refused to do any work until I got more men notwithstanding I have 35 in number [in line with] *the ships articles. Talked to them on the poop and fancied I had convinced them of their error.*
However, when it came to carrying out orders all the new ones

still refused to work. Alexander was very annoyed and wrote the following day:

Thursday 16th November 1848

At 3.45 a.m turned the hands out to heave the anchor up when all the sail men including Roberts and Homes positively refused to get the ship underway. Struck the Best Bower anchor, line short and made sail on the ship and at 7 weighed with the wind. westerly and made out between the heads. At 7.30 discharged Robert Jackson pilot. This will be sufficient I should imagine to show the ship could not be badly manned when with twelve able seamen in the Forecastle we got the ship underway from having two anchors down, in three hours' time. I omitted to mention that after the ship was fairly out to sea, I called these men on the poop and asked them if they were not ashamed of themselves as seamen to talk about the ship being short-handed as we could get the ship underway while twelve of them were in bed. At 2 p.m the men offered to turn to their posts, provided I would agree to discharge them in China which I readily agreed to and thought myself fortunate in having an opportunity of getting rid of such a confirmed set of blackguards.

Hiring sailors was a complex process. Some of the sailors on the *Charlotte Jane* may have signed on in London intending to stay on the ship for the duration of the voyage in order to secure their passage home. On arrival in Sydney some might abscond. Some might negotiate to stay in Sydney. Some may have signed on just as far as Australia. All needing to be replaced. Captains regularly employed fresh crews along the way, and needed to integrate them with those remaining.

Miriam did not mention anything about these difficulties and she was confused about the date they sailed from Sydney.

We sailed from Sydney sometime in February making the voyage to Hong Kong in about six weeks. The events that stand out in my memory are a fierce storm and a narrow escape from shipwreck.

About a week after leaving Sydney, one Sunday, almost everything unusual happens on a Sunday, we had our usual Sunday service on deck it being splendid weather. Far away on the horizon was a small cloud intensely black and big as a man's hand, the rest of the sky was perfectly clear. It appeared quite stationary. What little wind there was had quite died away. At three or so we were sitting down to dinner when in an instant the vessel healed over nearly onto her beam ends [sides nearly vertical] *sending the doctor, chair and all into the lee scuppers.* [metal lined cut away at the sides of ships to drain water away from the decks into the sea.] *Leg of mutton, goose, potatoes, plates, knives and forks and all following. The side of my bench kept me held in. My husband and mates went sprawling over the table but in the next instant had rushed on deck. The noise and confusion which followed may be imagined not described. The squall had come up sooner than anticipated. Indeed, it was a whirlwind.*

The ship had all sails set and it was hard work to make all snug in the teeth of the tremendous wind. The sky was black as night, the sea lashed to a foam and torrents of rain falling. Hearing something about waterspouts I managed to scramble on deck. There stood my husband at the helm and a sailor sitting beside him rubbing his head and looking much discomfited. The sky was black as ink with torrents of rain. Careering to leeward [the side opposite to that from which the wind is coming] *were no less than six huge waterspouts tearing up the sea, dancing up and down like black demons in the shape of black pipes tearing along through the sea. They look like great black spouts from sea to sky. They are really whirlwinds. One was close to the ship and another coming up behind. My husband said the sailor had lost his head and had been steering directly into one when my husband had dashed him down and taking the helm himself had steered just clear. The mate had got a gun and shot it and so dispersed it. This settled into a very severe gale which lasted a day or two. This is one of the many manifestations of Providence which I wish you to know as I tell you my life. Had the waterspout passed over the ship, the masts and sails would have been torn out of her and Grandmamma would not have been here to tell.*

Alexander recorded this event in the log book.

Sunday 19th November 1848.

10.30 a.m performed Divine Service. Lord Howe's Island distant 21 miles. light breeze from the Northward, rate of sailing 5 miles per hour Looking very heavy to the Southwest at 2 p.m getting very black to the southwest and lightening, a violent squall overtook the ship. Kept the ship right before the wind, a very strong whirlwind close on the starboard quarter and coming up fast tearing up the water furiously. Kept the ship up as much as possible to keep out of it but was afraid of the mast going. It rained heavily and then moderated. At 6 p.m rainier, steering to clear Elizabeth reef.

Alexander did not mention the gun shot or there being several waterspouts or the sailor who lost his nerve and was dashed down by Alexander. Whatever may or may not have happened I have included Miriam's version in full because it is so excitingly written and would have appealed to her grandchildren! I believe it was common practise to shoot into a waterspout and it was definitely thought to be a helpful thing to do though I gather there is little evidence now that it worked.

Alexander continued:

Monday 20th November 1848

A.m dark and gloomy weather with much lightning. At 6 p.m passed over the shoal called Golden grove without seeing any appearance of shoal water from the masthead. Keeping a good lookout for Middleton reef.

Sundays were meant to be days of rest for the crew who understandably, jealously guarded their time off. As long as the weather was good and everything in order the crew were only required to carry out minimal essential duties. On such Sundays there was often a holiday atmosphere on board ship with crew members relaxing, pursuing their own hobbies and pastimes or catching up with chores such as clothes washing, mending, getting a haircut or having a wash. Sundays for Captains were perhaps frustrating days as they may have wanted to get on as fast as possible with the voyage. Miriam does not tell us whether she allowed Helen to have the day off nor whether she herself took Sundays literally as a day of rest, doing no chores and perhaps only reading the Bible.

Thursday 30th November 1848.

A.m moderate wind from S.E. Steering North rate of sailing 7 miles per hour. A current this 24 hours, 1 mile an hour. The carpenter and his mate have been employed since we left Sydney in caulking and hardening the seams of the poop and examining them thoroughly also in the cabins and filling the seams with putty mixture of pitch. They will go on with main and lower decks.

Meanwhile Miriam wrote:

The China Sea through which we sailed was very superficially surveyed. There are many islands and they were not correctly laid down in the charts. One night my husband seemed very uneasy and I heard him remark that the chart was not to be relied on. A short time after I heard him give the order that all men were to be at their stations ready to haul the ship that night, that means to be ready to put the ship about or turn her round. The nurse, baby and I went to our berths as usual when about midnight we were awakened by a loud and terrible cry, "breakers ahead." [breakers are waves broken up by the presence of rocks on which ships can get wrecked] *The terror caused by this cry can only be understood by those like us on board ship in mid ocean. It being night increased the horror. All the watch below rushed on deck. In an instant every man was at work putting the ship about. All was noise and confusion, Grandpa's* [Alexander's] *and the mate's voices heard above the din. All were terrified, order upon order being given. On hearing that terrible cry and not knowing what to expect, poor Helen and I had thrown on a few clothes. I snatched baby Harriet out of her little bed and took a blanket in which to wrap her and we rushed into the cabin, where we sat pale and trembling. We found the doctor who strove to calm our fears. I looked out through the saloon window and saw a short distance astern a long line of white foam surf breaking on some low-lying shore. In an instant all were at work pulling the ship about.*

Alexander observed in the log book.

15th December 1848

A.m fresh breeze. Rate of sailing between 9$\frac{1}{2}$ and 10$\frac{1}{2}$ miles per hour. Noon. The island Poulesants [now known as *PULUSUK*] *63 miles distant. At 6 p.m went to the mast head and saw very low land lying 12 miles distant. Had everything made clear for working the ship. Stationed a hand on the fore yard, and an officer on the forecastle to look out. At 10 p.m being nearly in mid channel between* Pulusuk *and Enderby Island kept off to get into Mortlake tracks. Being past all foreseen danger set the Royals and Flying Jib but had only been 9 miles on the above course till a quarter past eleven p.m when I remarked to N. Stewart who was along with myself keeping a vigilant look out, that I did not like the appearance of a few seas which rolled passed and which had every appearance of a ground swell. Scarcely were the words spoken when the water suddenly became smooth. Ordered the lead* [instrument to tell water depth] *to be thrown overboard and while N. Stewart was in the act of sounding. I observed broken water about 2 or 3 cables length* [a cable is one-tenth of a sea mile] *on the weather bow which was immediately confirmed by N. Stewart. The hands who were warned to be in readiness were as instantly at their stations and the ship came round in an incredibly short space considering that she must have been going at the rate of 8$\frac{1}{2}$ or 9 miles per hour. Hauled the main sail up and furled* [rolled up and bound neatly] *the royals and flying jib and stationed the hands for going out again. Keeping the lead constantly going got bottom immediately. After the ship was round at 20 fathoms, hard coral bottom. Stood out nearly opposite to the course we came in, getting a bottom at 40 to 70 fathoms. At 10 past midnight after standing on that course 3 or 4 miles, breakers on the lee bow, was called by the look out on the fore yard. Down helm and although there was a good swell the ship came round beautifully.*

16th December 1848

2 a.m having made 6$\frac{1}{2}$ miles laid the main topsail to the mast until daylight Drifting 2 miles per hour. Thus, we had a most providential escape from being shipwrecked. Then came the thoughts of *deliverance from murder by the savages or lingering out a miserable existence in open boats.*

While I cannot excuse, those who were looking out forward and who ought to have seen the changes first, I cannot help remarking that great praise is due to both officers and men, especially N. Stewart for the coolness and attention with which every order was executed. At daylight fitted the main yard, Enderby Island then in sight distant 14 miles.

P.m went to the mast head but could see nothing of Pigalle Island took in all stud sails, Royals and Flying Jib and reefed the top sails and stood out under easy sail keeping a hand on the foreyard and two hands on the forecastle to look out. Midnight very squally and being well clear of anything laid down on the chart went and laid down not having been to bed for two nights.

Alexander's log book style was usually matter of fact, so this event must have been very serious for him to have written so emotionally, He appeared very pleased with the flexibility of the *Charlotte Jane* to turn around so neatly and quickly. I like to think he might have felt some satisfaction with the rigging he may have argued for when the ship was being built.

Those recalcitrant men taken on in Sydney appear to have done their work well under fear of death. They would have had to work very hard over those two nights tacking the ship this way and that. Though may be some of them were the ones who failed to spot the changes in the appearance of the water quickly enough.

Miriam also wrote with great relief

The good ship was saved. She answered her helm well and went round in almost less time than it takes to tell and the dreaded breakers were behind us. Your Grandpapa [Alexander] told me afterwards that we had been within a cable's length of the breakers and had the men not been at their posts we must have gone ashore on what proved to be, at daylight, a long low island inhabited most probably by savages as smoke was observed.

My husband afterwards sent a note to the Admiralty about this Island with Latitudes and Longitudes and it was put down in the Charts. When the ship was made snug again things quieted down and we went back to bed thankful we had been preserved from so great a danger and thanking that kind providence who so carefully watched over us.

Alexander noted

This most dangerous and I should say most extensive reef is not laid down in any chart and very much in the way of ships taking that passage which ought to be articled especially at night.

Sunday 17th December 1848

At 10.30 performed Divine Service and returned thanks to almighty God for our deliverance from Shipwreck.

Tuesday 19th December 1848.

One of the horses died this morning. Got him on deck and skinned him and threw him overboard.

I think Miriam may have been sad about this as she liked the horses. Perhaps Harriet was too as she may have visited them sometimes and even gingerly patted them.

Thursday 21st December1848

Daylight put all clear for painting inside and commenced after breakfast. P.m moderate breeze with passing showers which are very unpleasant when having been painting.

I suppose Alexander meant that the new paint had a strong smell which was unpleasant when the windows and doors were kept shut due to the rain; and I am thinking of the difficulty of keeping a toddler out of the way of painters and wet paint! Painting of the ship inside and more seriously outside was a never-ending activity as it would have been vital to preserve the wood.

Friday 22nd December 1848

A.m moderate and fine clear weather. Busily painting inside.

Saturday 23rd December

Moderate and fine clear weather all possible sail set rate of sailing 8½ miles per hour. Daylight cleared away for painting on the Poop. [Raised part at back of ship]

Sunday 24th December 1848.

Midnight strong gales.

Neither the log book nor Miriam's memoir make any mention of Christmas but I imagine that all on board ship would have been aware of the date and thinking of loved ones back home and celebrating. They were fortunate to be passing some islands actually on Christmas Day which would have added a bit of extra interest to the day.

Wednesday 27th December 1848

Daylight. In 24 fathoms of water amongst a great many fishing boats.

Thursday 28th December 1848.

Rate of sailing 4½ miles per hour at 5 a.m the land in sight. A pilot hauled up for the eastern passage into Hong Kong. At 10 a.m calm and variable Noon same weather. At 2 p.m got a breeze, at 3 p.m anchored in Hong Kong harbour with Larboard Bower anchor, abreast of Spring Gardens 40 cables out. Here ends the passage.

At this point it has been necessary to alter the order of events in the memoir, because Miriam muddled the two visits they made to Hong Kong. I have placed them in the correct order to fit with the log book.

She described their arrival in Hong Kong looking out of her port hole with great delight.

At the end of six weeks, we arrived off the Island of Hong Kong. I looked out of my window and saw great black mountains looming before us, very good. We were hauled to, waiting for the Chinese Pilot who presently came alongside us in a Chinese boat which you may be sure I attentively observed. I was much amused at hearing your grandpapa talk some Cantonese to him and hearing Pigeon English and at the dress of the old fellow who took us through the Chin water into Hong harbour. Several boats and Chinese Junks made their appearance. The Junks are very picturesque with their large yellow sails and red sides. They have large black eyes painted on each side of the bow. For the Chinese say "No hab eyes no can see, no can see how can make walkee.." I thought the scenery beautiful and the rock on which Hong Kong stands is very grand.

We took a walk through the town of Hong Kong which in those days was a small one then only consisting of one street and only possessing one road to the Happy Valley. We went to see the river course, the drive to which, through the Happy Valley was very pretty and I remember had a pretty waterfall. I remember it was some festival and a great firing of crackers and flying of red papers was going on and also flying of kites which the Chinese make in the form of dragons and birds and fly very cleverly.

In the native part of town, we saw open stalls on which were laid out for sale and I suppose to eat, baked dog, roast cat, numbers of rats strung by their tails onto sticks and other indescribable horrors.

The boat population is very curious. I was told that numbers of these people never go ashore but spend their entire lives on board the boats or sampans as they are called. The boats have a kind of telescopic arrangement of bamboo covers to make them completely private at night. In the day they are shoved right off in under the larger one, which thus then forms a shade from the sun. All the bedding, utensils and clothing is stowed into the hold and the deck replaced and covered with reed matting. This forms the floating house for all the family. They had a comical arrangement for taking care of the small children. An empty gourd was tied onto their backs with a piece of thin rope fastened to their waists, this attached to a small peg in the boat. If the creature fell overboard which often happened, the gourd prevented it sinking and it could be easily pulled on board again. They looked the oddest objects with their shaven crowns and little pigtails sticking straight from their heads. All kinds of domestic arrangements were carried on in these boats. In one you might see a father and mother seated, smoking quietly surrounded by their little ones. In another a full toilet might be proceeding. In another a woman would be combing out her ebony tresses or pencilling eyebrows or rouging cheeks. These boats were all quite close together and extended a long distance so that one could almost walk along from one to the other. If the wind blew, they banged against each other in an alarming fashion. The noise of screeching and quarrelling was terrific. On the borders of this strange fleet hovered a number of small punts, sufficiently long to contain a man, clothed only in a loin cloth and an immense umbrella shaped hat. In wet weather they would wear the hats and petticoats of long grass with bare legs regardless of appearances which were ludicrous. Many of these people got their living by laundry work for the shipping. Some of the punts would be filled with fruit or maybe a cat or two demurely sitting tied by thin ropes around their necks or perhaps a wretched dog or two or some parrots. They were a kind of provision merchant to the boat people who mostly live on fish and rice. While lying here we had a visit from Mr Bursus, the missionary of the Presbyterian Church. This, now prosperous, was then in its infancy. Accompanying my old missionary were six Chinese boys about seventeen or so and full of curiosity about the ship. Mr Bursus had adopted the Chinese costume and lived with these boys in Chinese fashion in order to more readily gain their confidence.

We do not know what happened to the cargo of horses but I think the Hong Kong racecourse may have recently been opened so perhaps they were taken for racing or breeding. Indeed, Miriam and Alexander received an invitation from the Hong Kong committee to attend a ball. This was found amongst Miriam's papers. Was it kept because of some now unknown importance or mere chance that it has remained all these years?

The log book continued after a five week stay in Hong Kong.

Ship Charlotte Jane from Hong Kong to Singapore.

Friday 2nd February 1849

At 4 p.m gave my papers came on board and weighed anchor set all plain sailing and struck out of Hong Kong. At 8 p.m discharged the pilot. At 9.30 the Asses Ears distant 4½ miles.

Sunday 4th Feb 1849

Midnight clear moonlight weather.

Tuesday 6th Feb 1849

I observe that a current must have been setting to the N E at the rate of 1½ miles per hour.

Wednesday 7th Feb 184

At 4 a.m was called out of bed by N. Juguel, he having seen broken water, immediately ran on deck and on the starboard beam about a quarter of a mile off I saw the sea breaking heavily over a rock about a ships length tho' nothing of rock appeared above water. Took in all stud sails and hauled the ship to the wind for a little but immediately kept away again.

There are many islands in this area but Alexander was not clear which islands he was seeing. It appears that the charts differed as to the position of a particular shoal. The log continued:

Midnight keeping a good look out for a reef seen by the Bombay Castle and also 'Charlotte Banks Survey' by Captain Bass. Sounded several times but had never less than 30 fathoms."

Thursday 8th Feb 1849

A.m keeping a good look out, a hand on the fore yard and two on the Forecastle. Daylight nothing in sight. Midnight clear moonlight.

Saturday 10th Feb 1849

A.m moderate and fine weather. At 1 p.m anchored in Singapore roads in 4½ fathoms water. 40 fathoms cable out.

Miriam was as excited as ever to be arriving at a new destination.

We arrived at the lovely island of Singapore, looking like an emerald set in a turquoise sea. Much did I enjoy the delicious fruits, especially the pineapples and mangosteen which is lovely to look at. It is like a divided pearl lying on a crimson cushion enclosed in an ebony casket.

While in Singapore an amusing adventure befell us. A friend Mr Mi invited us to spend the day at his place, a short distance from the town. My husband was to join us in the evening. Accordingly, he put us into a Garry telling the Garry Waller where we were to go. The Garry Waller sometimes running beside us and sometimes riding on the shafts, we rode on for about an hour and I asked him if he knew his way as we were now going through the jungle. "Oh yes Memsahib." So, on we went for some time further. Knowing the house was only a short distance from the town I became uneasy, but the man told me he knew the house well. Presently we drove through a grove of nutmeg trees and came to a large house. The door was opened by an old Chinaman who told me Mr Mi lived there. So, I got out of the Garry and was shown up to a large suite of rooms. I entered. They appeared as if they had not been used lately but Mr Mi being a widower, I thought explained it. I explained to the man who I was and that Mr Mi expected me. He hastened to get me water and by and bye he brought us a nice luncheon and said I could stay as long as I liked. So, we made ourselves cosy and settled down to wait for my husband.

Time passed and no husband came.

This must have been very frightening for Miriam, to arrive after a much longer trip than expected and then find that Mr Mi was not at home would have been nerve wracking enough, but then to wait nearly all day would have become really worrying.

I wonder what sort of food supplies Miriam might have brought with her for Harriet to eat and drink? Would Helen have tried to cheer up her mistress or would she have felt it was not her place? Perhaps she would have been too irritated and scared to do anything.

Whatever the case, they would both have been wondering what on earth to do. Miriam continued:

I looked out onto the compound and saw two gentlemen talking and looking up anxiously at the window. It was getting dark and I was feeling very uneasy, when suddenly appeared at the further end of the garden two gentlemen on ponies riding as fast as possible. As they came nearer, I knew they were my husband and Mr Mi. They looked very hot and disturbed.

I hurried down to them and found I had come to the wrong house and there were two Mr Mi's. When they had gone to Mr Mi's house to their horror, they had found that I was not there. As tigers were about in the jungle the dreadful idea got into their heads that we had been eaten. Someone then suggested that we might have gone to the wrong house. They procured two ponies and galloped off as hard as they could and great was my husband's joy when finding his wife and baby safe. The gentleman to whose house we had gone, kindly had dinner prepared for us. The old Chinaman thinking there was some mistake had thought his mistress had returned. She being expected then.

Strangely enough my daughter Harriet when grown up married one of the partners of the gentleman to whose house we had been taken.

This little event caused much amusement in Singapore and some verses about the Captain who lost his wife were inserted in the daily paper.

What a relief for Miriam and Helen to be safely reunited with Alexander and the right Mr Mi. Once all the real fear was over it would have been satisfying to be rescued in such a heroic manner by two gentlemen gallantly galloping on horseback, over part of the island to save them in the nick of time before the tigers came out to eat them!

Sometime during their visit to Singapore Miriam wrote a long and newsy letter to her parents, dated February 1848. This date is incorrect as by the time they were in Singapore 1849 was well under way! I understand that this is a common occurrence when people are on long voyages. Perhaps time seems endless and is therefore difficult to be accurate about. Certainly, in the log book the following year, Alexander continued writing 1849 until 19th January 1850 and then for the next few days had to keep making corrections!

Ship Charlotte Jane

Singapore

February 1848

My dear Mama and Papa,

We have been one week here, it is, notwithstanding the heat, a most delightful place. It is very warm indeed; it is just impossible to do anything in the middle of the day. Very early in the morning and in the evening are the only times but the best of it is it is always the same. No sudden changes. Hong Kong is a dreadful place for that. One day boiling hot the next day piercing cold. We have been staying ashore all the week and have seen pretty much of the country. It is really very pretty though very infested with tigers. It is not safe to walk out after dark.

We used to get up very early in the morning about half past five, daybreak, and get everything done before the heat of the day. The ladies here generally go out in the morning and then we had tiffin at one o'clock, took a siesta all afternoon, dined at five and then out for a drive all the rest of the evening. Every lady keeps a Garry, a sort of double seated cab and the man runs at the horses head all the way, never drives, but wherever you go there runs the man, very fast leading the horse and they don't seem to feel the fatigue at all. Men here wear the Indian dress just a white cloth thrown around them in a very graceful manner and a white turban. It is very cool and simple. Gentlemen here dress entirely in white. Alick has kept a Garry all the time and we have had a nice drive every evening. You get the finest pineapples here in the world such large ones so very different from those we get in England. I was at a gentleman's the other day who has a very large plantation of nutmegs.

We have one or two. Also, some peppers and I also saw the tobacco shrub, the cashew nut, cocoa nuts, by the way this is the place for cocoa nuts you get them as big as your hand. [I am not sure if she means coconuts?] I forgot to tell you that pineapples here cost two cents a -piece or fifty for a dollar. I am tired of them we have had so many!

Two ships came in today from Calcutta with the news that our troops are beaten on the Punjab by the Sikhs and they turned back and ran away. These are your British troops. This is the true news, but the government do not wish it to be known and so it is given out here that we have gained a victory. They fired a salute this morning upon the receipt of the news to make believe it was something to rejoice about. You will have the news by the mail that brings this.

[Fake news was obviously around then too!]

Where do you think I was last night? at the theatre. There was an amateur performance by all the gentlemen. The Officers and merchants and the Manager wished us very much to go. So, we went full dressed of course like everyone else and it is so unusual here to see a strange lady that everyone was wondering who we were. The very absurdity of the acting and dresses made it something I was much amused by, for you know anything of that sort is new to me.

My little baby is quite well she has six teeth and runs quite alone about everywhere keeping me in a constant fidget. She is growing taller but is rather thin I suppose that is because of the heat but she seems very well. She wears nothing but one of those little pincloth aprons. Her mind is very sharp she is making great efforts to talk. I am very well and so is Alick and so is Ellen. She [baby] is extremely amusing. We have had three monkeys on board she does not so much like them. We went into a shop the other day with all sorts of queer and pretty Chinese things in it. She looked round for a great while half frightened when all at once she began to chatter and caper in Ellen's arms and put out her hands and took up a queer looking Chinese joss made of china with its tongue sticking out and making a most charming countenance. So of course, as she took a fancy to it her Papa must buy it for her and nothing has pleased her so much for a very long while.

The mate has just given into my care a box containing three thousand five hundred and thirty-nine dollars it is very small but so heavy I can hardly lift it.

[I like to think Miriam wrote this thinking that her younger brothers and sisters would have been intrigued' by this information.]

I hope you are all well. Give my fondest love to all my brothers and sisters and the same yourselves from me, very dear Papa and Mama. Alick sends the same.

Your truly affectionate daughter Minnie A Lawrence

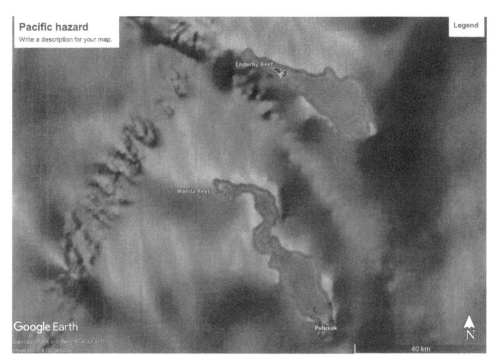

Google Earth image of sea between Pulusuk and Enderby, showing centre below in strong blue shallow underwater reef stretching NW from Pulusuk island, a hazard not fully charted in 1848 when the *Charlotte Jane* narrowly avoided being wrecked on Manila reef. (Image by Google Earth; Data SIO. NOAA. U.S.Navy. NGA.GEBCO; Image–EC181.60 Landsat/ Copernicus)

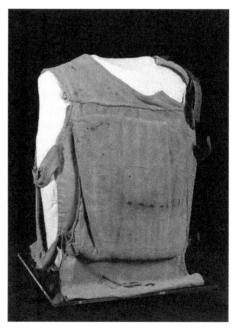

Life Jacket used on the *Charlotte Jane*, canvas with leather straps and metal buckles. (Barker collection, Canterbury Museum, Christchurch, NZ; image 1948.23.1)

Hong Kong from Kow-loon, drawn by Thomas Allom, sketched on the spot by
Capt. Stoddart RN, engraved by S.Fisher, from 'China Illustrated 1843-1847'.
(supplied by Steve Bartrick Antique prints and maps)

Hong Kong street, chromolithograph by Hilderbrandt, early 1860s.

A sampan (modern photograph)

'Kite flying at Hae-kwan, on the Ninth Day of the Ninth Moon', drawn by Thomas Allom, engraved by A.Willmore. (supplied by Steve Bartrick Antique prints and maps)

Boat People, Hong Kong c.1870 (reproduced by permission of the Government of the HKSAR from the collection of the Hong Kong Museum of History; image P1970.44)

Singapore, engraved by A.H.Payne after a picture by C.Graham published in 'The Chinese Empire', circa 1858 (supplied by Steve Bartrick Antique prints and maps)

Singapore waterfront from the sea 1840s (courtesy National Archives of Singapore; image19980005124-0119)

Singapore "when tigers used to roam" (by bit.ly)

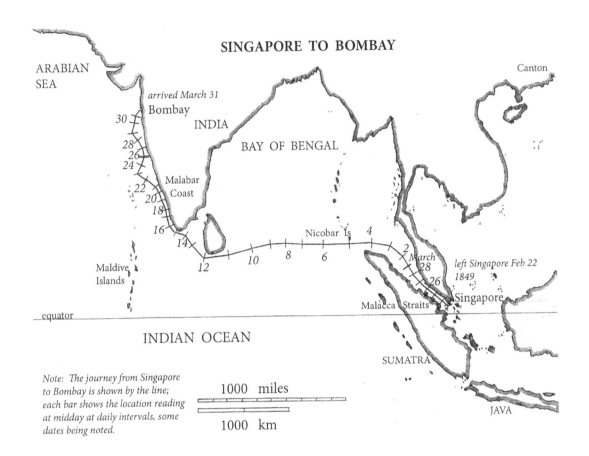

SINGAPORE TO BOMBAY

ARABIAN SEA

Canton

arrived March 31

30

Bombay

INDIA

28
26
24

BAY OF BENGAL

Malabar Coast

22

20

18

16

14

Nicobar Is   4

March
28

2

12   10   8   6

left Singapore Feb 22
1849

26

Maldive Islands

Singapore

Malacca Straits

equator

INDIAN OCEAN

SUMATRA

Note: The journey from Singapore
to Bombay is shown by the line;
each bar shows the location reading
at midday at daily intervals, some
dates being noted.

1000 miles

1000 km

JAVA

BOMBAY.

Bombay Fort, steel engraving by Allom and Willmore, 1858
(supplied by Steve Bartrick Antique prints and maps)

Chapter 4

SINGAPORE TO BOMBAY
38 days at sea

Miriam wrote:

We only remained a week in Singapore [12 days] *to allow pilgrims to embark and to take in a cargo of opium and onions. The combined odour was somewhat overwhelming.* [This is interesting but I think Miriam is not correct. If they were carrying opium it would be more likely on their way back from India where opium was grown.]

We again set sail this time for Bombay. We had a full complement of pilgrims on board or Hadji, also a Persian Gentleman and two Hindoo ladies, who poor things were taken down below carefully covered up in shawls and not brought up till we arrived in Bombay, when they were well covered up from profane eyes. The Persian was a fine-looking man who carried about him a quantity of sugar candy with which he constantly fed the baby. [How shocking for us today to contemplate an almost unknown man liberally feeding a toddler sugar!] *He also sported an immense yellow silk handkerchief which he kept hanging over his shoulder and used to flick away flies. Whenever I appeared, he discreetly went to the other end of the deck. The Hadji were a strange wild looking set very constant in their prayers and devotions; spreading their carpets and performing various genuflections and prostrations, every morning and evening, in the middle of which, they would turn round and scold or have a little conversation and then continue their devotions. Their wild figures standing up against the red beams of the setting sun were very picturesque.*

The vessel was manned by Lascars [sailors from India or South East Asia.] *They also were wild and picturesque and on fine evenings we would hear the strumming of some kind of strange guitar accompanying a wild song. On fine Sundays they came out like gorgeous butterflies dressed in raiment fearful and wonderful to behold, but at the least hint of a drop of rain Hey Presto all was changed and they became veritable earthworms as they hastened to return to the dull brown garb of working days. They were commanded by a huge creature called the Serang. How he did beat them but they did not seem to care.*

The Lascars were contracted as a team through the Serangs who acted as brokers in ports and then as headmen on board ship. They were the translators and negotiators between the Lascars and the Ship's Master and her crew.

They were originally used in the East India Company. Alexander had probably employed them when he worked for his uncle who was an East Indian merchant, so it is not surprising that they were contracted onto the *Charlotte Jane.* They had a reputation for being skilful seamen. They were paid less than the British which of course made them very desirable to employers but perhaps looked down on by some crew members. Miriam seemed to be quite fascinated by them.

There is a strange discrepancy in this part of the voyage between the memoir and the log book. Alexander did not mention anything in the log book about taking on board a number of Pilgrims. I cannot imagine that the log book would not record what was happening with such a number of voyagers on board. I therefore conclude that Miriam may have been remembering some other voyage where she may have travelled with pilgrims on their way to Mecca. It could be possible that the Persian gentleman and his women passengers might have been on board. Miriam wrote so descriptively about him and his interactions particularly with Harriet. Remembering events from 40 years ago can never be totally accurate, and the pilgrims were not mentioned again.

Alexander did not mention anything about opium and onions either. There are however, several references in the log book about the Lascars so on that point both our sources are in agreement! Once again, I feel justified in including Miriam's descriptions as they are very colourful.

Miriam continued:

Our course lay through the Straits of Malacca. How lovely it all was. The weather was generally fine and deliciously warm. The wind sometimes being adverse, we had to tack and sail pretty close in shore. Once we went close to the town of Malacca looking very pretty with its white stone houses in the midst of tall palm trees and coconuts. Sometimes natives would come with their most beautiful boats filled with fruit or chicken or with an occasional monkey. Sometimes a boat with a strange outrigger and filled to overflowing with natives would come merrily dancing over the water and with a great amount of screeching and shouting they would fasten her alongside the ship and some would leap on deck and uncoiling a dirty piece of linen from round their loins would display in their brown palms, gold chains, brilliants and rings for sale. Sometimes they would have monkeys. If we declined to buy, they would spring to their heels and fly off like the wind.

If it had not been for the Sumatra squalls and the cockroaches, I should have been quite happy. The squalls were quite terrifying. A small black cloud would appear on the horizon and in a few minutes the sun would be blotted out and deluges of rain would come, afterwards followed by violent wind. Woe to the Captain who is not looking out. Away go the sails and everything, but they only last a short time and then the sun shines out in all her brilliancy.

The cockroaches were fearful. At 9 p.m regularly they would hold a grand parade coming out in myriads from all parts making a great rushing noise flying about and entangling themselves in one's hair, dropping into our tea and covering every place. I used to wrap myself entirely in a sheet, head and all. At the end of about a quarter of an hour they would disappear as quickly as they appeared. The Doctor showed me his toe and finger nails, gnawed to the quick by them and my baby had some hair eaten from the top of her head and made quite sore by them one night. I took care it should only happen once. The ants were capital [scavengers.] If they found one half dead, they quickly gnawed off his limbs then his head and wings and carried them off to their homes.

Little Harriet was now growing very amusing, noticing and mimicking everything. She was very fond of her Papa. She was a dear little thing. She was a great favourite with the mates and men who were all very fond of her. She was once seen I believe, smoking a pipe.

Miriam was correct that they sailed through the Malacca Straits, but they sailed through them on two occasions. She placed her descriptions the wrong way round. I have corrected this so that her writing fits with the log book.

Here is the record in the log book of this part of the voyage.

Tuesday 22nd February 1849

At 4 a.m made sail. At 5 let go from the Bury at which we had been laying for some days but it falling calm almost immediately let go the anchor to prevent getting foul of a Brig at anchor. The barque the Trusty in company. Midnight fine.

Leaving Singapore to sail to Bombay required careful navigation going through the Malacca Straits.

There were several ships going at the same time and islands and rocks to be avoided as well as shallow waters to be sounded for safe anchorage particularly at night.

Friday 23rd February 1849

At 7 anchored in 20 fathoms of water off shore 13 miles. Midnight wind off the land.

Saturday 24th February 1849

A.m weighed with the land wind and steered along the land for Cape Richard. Passed Cape Richard at 5 p.m anchored in 25 fathoms of water. Midnight light breeze off the land.

Sunday 25th February 1849

Light Breezes off the land at 2.30 a.m the Trusty *nearly ran into us although we had a light hoisted at the Starboard fore gall arm.*

Keeping ships lit during the hours of darkness and when foggy would have required constant attention as they would need regular maintenance and sufficient supplies of fuel. There must also have had to be strict regulations to avoid fires on board ship. Electricity being still in its infancy.

At 3 a.m weighed and steered to get off the land. It looking very squally to the Southward. At 7 p.m heavy rain, wind variable. After making several levels anchored in 20 fathoms of water to wait tide and daylight for crossing the North and South Sands.

Monday 26th February 1849

Daylight squally with very heavy rain. At 9 it cleared away a little. Weighed, it became quite thick again. Keeping the lead going. At 1 p.m shoaled the water to 11 – 12 or 15 fathoms supposed to be on the South Sand head.

From the mizen topmast they saw two other ships in the Straits and stood over towards them. It must have been difficult when the wind was blowing hard to avoid collisions.

At 2 p.m took in all sail and anchored with the Bower anchor in 12 fathoms water. Furled sails and set the Lee watch.

Tuesday 27th February 1849

Made sail with the tide. Tacking in mid channel.

The Trusty *at anchor on the South Sand.*

Wednesday 28th February 1949

Midnight making sundry tacks to weather the Islands and expecting to get the wind off the land

Thursday 1st March 1849

At daylight a ship on our weather beam supposed to be the Charlotte which left Singapore 2 days before us.

Alexander enjoyed knowing that another ship had made slower progress than the *Charlotte Jane*!

At 8 a.m squally off the land. At 11 spoke the ship Charlotte. At 2 p.m Capt. Thomas came on board. 3.30 p.m Captain Thomas went [back] on board. 11 p.m being close to the mud banks tacked the ship to the Westward. Midnight hazy weather.

Passing ships would signal each other to exchange information about where they had come from and where they were going and to check longitude and latitudes when possible. They also sometimes took mail in the small rowing boats from one ship to another if they were close enough and travelling in the right direction. Keeping a constant look out as to what ships were around and passing on information from ship to ship was very important as there were often pirates about.

Monday 5th March 1848

A.m light airs from the Eastward. Steering West, rate of sailing 2 miles per hour. At 6 breezes increasing a little and looking squally to the Eastward. At 9 saw the Great Nicobar Island. At 10.45 passed the South point 4 miles offshore. Noon. Latitude 6.41. Longitude by chronometer 93.48. Longitude by bearings of the South Point 93. 48. Rate of sailing at an average of 6 miles per hour.

Saturday 10th March 1849

I found today that the stern plate for the gig could not be found although sent on board in Singapore.

Sunday 11th March 1849

I have no doubt that a current has set us considerably to the Southward.

Thursday 15th March 1849

Nearly calm. Latitude Observation. 7.38 North. Longitude Chronometer 77.6 East, which is considerably farther to the westward than the bearings of the land, this I cannot account for as the chronometers were quite right at the Nicobar Islands.

Friday 16th March 1849

Boarded by a boat with salt fish and baskets for sale.

Saturday 17th March 1849

A.m squally at NW Tacked off shore about 3 miles, in 12 fathoms water. At 3 Tacked in shore. At 4 tacked off with the wind off the land. Daylight. The Seahorse in sight hull down astern and a Barque in sight on the weather bow. At noon Latitude observation 9.17. Longitude chronometer by bearing of the land 76.21. have gained considerably on both vessels at 2 p.m a ship in sight on starboard bow at 3 another in sight on starboard bow but cannot make out how she is going, at 5 another in sight on starboard bow standing the same way. Abreast of Alleppey about 10 miles off shore. Several large ships at anchor.

Sunday 18th March 1849 [Creeping along the Malabar Coast towards Mangalore.]

A.m light airs and calm. At 4 spoke to an Arab ship from Alleppey who said that the ships at anchor there were all Arab. All the coast here is laid down about 2 miles further East than it really is.

Alexander was very confused by the charts not being accurate. It must have been annoying and alarming to find you were not where you thought you were and frustrating to have been making such slow progress.

Thursday 22nd March 1849

The land all along here by Hausebury's charts is placed 14 to 20 miles farther than it really is so that our distance from the land is 54 miles.

This is further confirmation of the maps not being accurate.

P.m breeze increasing rate of sailing 6½ miles per hour. At 3 p.m tacked ship in shore. Lying NE at 10 tacked off. Midnight ship pitching a good deal with a heavy head sea.

Saturday 24th March 1849

At 1.30 a.m tacked ship to the Westward going very little through the water, there being a heavy head swell. Daylight Nothing in sight from the mast head.

Monday 26th March 1849

A.m light breeze gaining nothing through the water. At daylight two vessels in shore which have a little breeze and gaining on us. At 5 p.m the full-rigged ship has gained at least two miles since we first saw her and tho' she has had some little advantage over us she undoubtedly sails faster and being the first ship that has passed us I am very curious to know what she is. I may remark at the same time that on looking over the ship since the other day I observed a sheet of copper hanging off. I hope this is not the case anywhere else as it would not only retard the ship but compel us to put the ship in dock at Bombay. At 10.30 p.m tacked off, Greys Island about 2 miles. Midnight tacked in again.

Wednesday 28th March 1849

The ship that beat us so much in light wind is ahead but we are coming up fast. At 6 close- in shore signalled the clipper Sir Herbert Compton which left Singapore two days before us and which was to make a 20 days passage and take in Bombay at least a week under us.

*In this I guess Captain Brown will find himself disappointed and
I shall gain from him two hats. Tacked off shore. Ship plunging a
good deal against a heavy head sea. Midnight same weather.*

I am not sure what Alexander meant about gaining two hats but I know he
liked to gloat when he went faster than another vessel! So, this will have
cheered him up!

Thursday 29th March 1849

*A.m strong breeze with a heavy head sea. Ship labouring a good deal.
I find that two or three sheets of copper is off the ship larboard
beam and one or two started on the starboard side ahead of the
fore chains. Midnight tacked off the land in 12 fathoms water.*

Saturday 31st March 1849

*A.m light breeze. with a heavy head sea ship pitching a good deal
and only going to leeward. At 9 the breeze set in at North. Rate of
sailing 4½ to 5 miles per hour. Noon. Strong breeze with a heavy
head sea. Ship pitching a good deal. P.m strong breeze at 6.30
received a pilot on board. At 9 anchored. Lowered the sails down
and set a sea hotel. Here ends this passage.*

Chapter 5

STAYING IN BOMBAY

Arriving in Bombay after a somewhat tricky passage must have been exciting for everyone on the *Charlotte Jane*.

Miriam wrote:

We reached Bombay in safety. The town looked grand from the harbour which was filled with shipping and there was a fine-looking palace with a great many steps. They call it the Ghat.

Miriam wrote a rather perplexed letter to her mother soon after arriving in Bombay. She was even more out of date with the year as she still wrote 1848!

Ship Charlotte Jane
April 2nd 1848

My dear Mama,

This letter ought to have been sent by the last mail but by some means was forgotten, but you will have heard from Alick where we were coming, as he wrote to Papa from Singapore. If you wish to write and I hope you will for I long to hear how you are all. Getting an address to

Messrs Turner and Company

Hong Kong

You may also if you can write me immediately address one to

Messrs Ritchie, Stoward and Company

Bombay

But you would need to write here directly you receive this so that I might get it by next mail before we leave. Harriette [sister] might write as I know you cannot always do so when you wish and I suppose by this time she is quite au fait at everything of that sort. She must be growing quite a young woman. They must all be growing big now. I should like to see you all again. It will be a long time yet, though we have had a very pleasant voyage from Singapore. It is excessively warm here. I hate the warm weather I don't feel fit for anything.

Will you tell Elizabeth to write to Ellen or one of them, at the same time you write to me, as she wants a letter very badly. I am sorry to say that Ellen is very far from improving. The only thing is she is kind to the child who is fond of her.

Our decks just now are looking very picturesque. The people about in their eastern dress, it is a very pretty dress with the long flowing white robes and the gay coloured turbans. We have only been here two or three days so I have not yet been ashore but I will write to you again by the next mail and tell you all about it. We are all very well. Alick sends his kind love to all. Little baby is trotting about everywhere she is growing extremely passionate. One thing is that she is just about getting her eye teeth. Give my kind love to all my brothers and sisters and accept the same yourself my dear Mama from your truly affectionate daughter.

Minnie A Lawrence

This length of time not hearing anything is unimaginable to us nowadays when we can communicate all over the world in seconds. Poor Miriam, she must have been worried that something might have happened to the family or else felt they could not be bothered to write. Helen had not had any letters either, so they were both in the same boat and possibly pretty fed up with each other too!

Miriam wrote:

A friend of my husband carried us all off to stay in his house, a little way out of the town. Their house stood in a large piece of ground overlooking gardens, called a compound. It was very large with immense rooms, very lofty, so much so that there were bird's nests in the corners. There were no doors only screens, no windows only green jalousies. [shutters.] *The immense rooms, the semi-darkness, the white robed servants moving noiselessly about all seemed to me like a dream. We used to wake up at about 4 a.m when a cup of tea was brought to us. Then we went back to bed again. Most people went out for a drive at about 5. After the gentlemen had left for the town, we ladies sat in the great outer room where the monotony was sometimes varied by an Indian pedlar making his appearance. They would enter unannounced, and making a low salaam greeting would squat on the ground and proceed to unroll their huge bundles to display magnificent shawls worth £100 or £200 a piece, muslin, oriental slippers, gold bangles, chains and precious stones. I thought I had got into the Arabian Nights. On our deciding not to buy they would quickly fold all up again and depart with a low salaam.*

[£100s would have been a huge amount of money in those days].

In the evening we drove through the bazaar as the narrow streets were called. The Parsee women in their bright robes, the white robed turbaned men, the dark skinned Hindoo peasant women moving gracefully along with burdens poised on their heads, the pedlars seated before their wares, brilliant blue sky and here and there a splendid mosque, white as snow, standing against the azure, all combined to make in my unaccustomed eyes, a scene on which I never tired gazing. Through these crowds our carriage and pair would be rapidly driven. The way being cleared by two white robed servants running before us shouting, "Gulla Walla, get out of the way." And I saw many novel sights. Bombay was not then the city I hear it has become. The shops were more like wooden booths than anything else and the merchant squatted amongst his goods. The streets were crowded with a variety of passengers, vehicles and pedestrians mingling in picturesque confusion. In one part there was a small white washed temple in which could be dimly discerned an ugly idol. The first time I saw men devoutly kneeling and worshipping before this piece of clay I felt sick. We generally passed a place where was a large well, round which numbers of women waited for their turn to draw water. They were mostly dressed in different coloured satin robes, green, yellow, blue and crimson, with veils of the same, hanging at the back of their heads and a broad band of white linen concealing their hair and part of the forehead. They had bare feet and arms with gold bangles and anklets. They were handsome with large black eyes and eyebrows. When their pots were filled, they lifted them onto their heads and walked away with the gait of a queen. The poorer women have roll upon roll of blue cloth around their loins, the men nothing but a bit of cloth round the loins, the children roll on the ground naked. On the esplanade the beauty and fashion of Bombay congregated and here the Parsees came. The ladies in little covered carriages of red cloth carefully concealed from public view. These were drawn by pretty little buffaloes. The great fat men lolled in their carriages clothed in light filmy coloured cotton coats and their peculiar conical caps. The children are lovely and were beautifully dressed in gold spangled muslins and satin and jewels. We drove home by the sea shore, the red beams of the setting sun casting a lovely light over the rocks.

One Sunday night returning from Church we met a Hindoo wedding procession. A pretty boy about eight years old, gaily dressed in muslin, was sitting in a silver saddle on a white horse. He was holding in his arms a lovely little girl a year or two, younger fast asleep. This was the bride and groom. A number of white robed men went in front with musical instruments and flaming torches. Surrounding them were a number of women wearing brilliant-coloured satin robes and more men with torches.

They passed with a great deal of noise and flare and glitter.

Another time we went to see something of a Hindoo wedding ceremony. We walked through the compound. The glow worms were trying to outshine the moon. When we came to the house, we saw a number of turbaned men seated under the veranda at regular intervals, each a little lamp before them and some betel nuts.

We were taken to see the bride, after being deluged with rose water out of silver flagons and presented with betel nut wrapped in gilt covered leaves. The bride was a pretty looking girl dressed in spangled muslin and lots of bangles and jewels. In her nose was a ring with splendid pearls and emeralds. She looked rather bewildered, tired and dazed, though

*she smiled when we presented her jewels. She was surrounded by
chattering women.*

*Another day we saw a Parsee funeral. The body was on an open bier
decked with white flowers and borne by four bearers. A few others were
escorting it to the tower of silence, as these people call the towers on
which the body is laid on a grating. As the body decays it falls through
into the hole underneath or is carried away by the vultures that are always
in waiting.*

*We made an excursion for my benefit to the caves of Elephanta, taking
with us a hamper of good things. We got into a large covered boat like a
house, with a sail and rowers and went off to the Island. The tide being out
the boat could not go close to the shore so I had to accomplish the difficult
feat of getting out of the boat and into a covered palanquin in which one
can only lie down. We were in the middle of the water and there was such
a chasm that one might fall between the two boats. I managed to roll in
somehow but with much discomposure of dress.* [What a very plucky
woman Miriam was. Here she was about 6 months pregnant in the boiling
heat, off on a day's excursion kitted out in a great long ankle length dress,
clambering and wriggling about from one wobbling boat to another.
Undaunted!]

She continued:

*The caves are very extensive and wonderful with carved images of Gods
and Goddesses everywhere and splendid columns. They made me wonder
at the number and hideousness of the heathen gods and made me thankful
that for me there is only one God and that one a kind and merciful one.*

Miriam stated that this expedition was set up especially for her but she
did not say who organised it for her. Perhaps Alexander had a hand in it
through contacts he may have made during the years he used to sail to
India earlier in his career. Miriam seemed so eager to see as much as
possible and learn about other people and their cultures and religions.
Some of her responses however may seem to us nowadays rather
prejudiced. She seemed eager to venture out on her own and Alexander
was not against her going out unaccompanied by him.

One of the prettiest sights I remember seeing in Bombay was that of the Parsees salaaming the new moon on the Esplanade which they did with great apparent devoutness. There are in Bombay a set of men called Ceedies. As black and shiny as ebony, of gigantic size, splendidly proportioned. They are chiefly employed as porters about the wharfs.

Part of the time in Bombay I lived on the ship which I liked quite as well as on shore. The ship's provider never failed to bring me a little posy of roses which was laid beside my plate at breakfast. Whenever you pay a visit to the Hindoo they throw rose water over you out of small silver vases, rather startling the first time you experience it.

I will mention one curious thing, we always dined at 7 o'clock regularly. As we sat down three frogs hopped in and took their seats under a small table at regular distances and sat quietly all the time of dinner and quietly hopped out again. Why they came or what they got no one could tell.

I like to think that Miriam included this little snippet about the frogs to amuse her younger grandchildren.

I was rather glad to leave Bombay as it was becoming very hot. I could not tie my bonnet strings without perspiring profusely. Harriet and Helen were nearly devoured by the mosquitoes.

While in Bombay the ship had to have the copper panels re-fixed as Alexander had feared. When that was finally completed the *Charlotte Jane* set sail on 16th May 1849 for Canton, China via Singapore and Hong Kong. What cargo she carried we do not know for certain, but this seems the most likely time for her to be carrying the opium and possibly the onions, that Miriam mentioned earlier.

Caves of Elephanta island, near Bombay. (courtesy Government Art Collection; image GAC16152)

Scene in Bombay, behind St. Thomas church, by Robert Grindlay and
R.G.Greeve, 1826. (courtesy British Library)

View near Harbour Gate, looking north along Apollo Street, Bombay,
with Scotch church built 1819 on left; lithograph circa 1843.

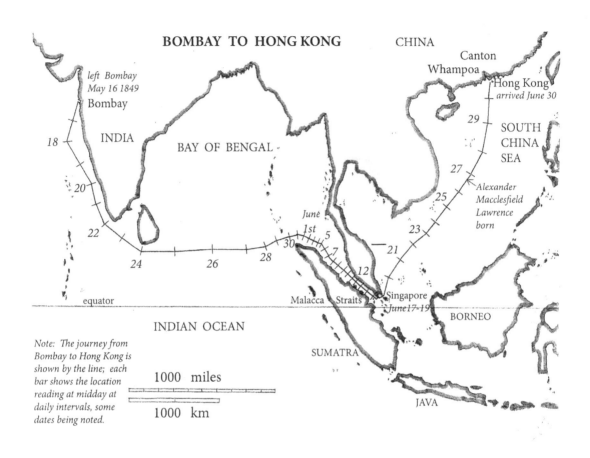

BOMBAY TO HONG KONG

*left Bombay
May 16 1849*
Bombay

INDIA

18

20

22

24   *26*   *28*

BAY OF BENGAL

equator

INDIAN OCEAN

*Note: The journey from
Bombay to Hong Kong is
shown by the line; each
bar shows the location
reading at midday at
daily intervals, some
dates being noted.*

1000 miles

1000 km

*June
1st*   5

30   7

12

Malacca   Straits

SUMATRA

JAVA

CHINA

Canton
Whampoa
Hong Kong
arrived June 30

29

SOUTH
CHINA
SEA

27

25

*Alexander
Macclesfield
Lawrence
born*

23

21

Singapore
June 17–19

BORNEO

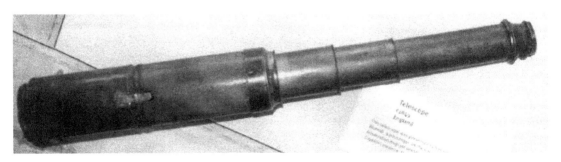

Telescope used by Captain Lawrence who presented it to Samuel Wornall, passenger, circa 1849.
(courtesy the Canterbury Museum, Christchurch, New Zealand; image 1957.25.1)

Chapter 6

FROM BOMBAY TO
HONG KONG VIA SINGAPORE

33 days at sea and 2 days in Singapore

The log book re opened on:

May 16th 1849

A.m light breezes from the Westward. At 4 made sail. At 5.30 John Anderson Pilot came on board and at 6 weighed from the middle ground and worked out of the harbour. Rate of sailing 5 miles per hour. Ship very tender. Midnight moderate and fine.

[The ship being tender means that the ship may have a tendency to lean over due to the cargo being unevenly balanced. Perhaps she held opium.]

The Memoir continued:

We bade our kind friends farewell and set sail again for China. This time going through the Malacca straits was more tedious. We had light head winds but the weather was lovely.

Alexander noted:

May 23rd 1849

An increasing breeze from the Westward with frequent light squalls and showers. I consider the Monsoon has regularly set in.

Whilst the *Charlotte Jane* was anchored amongst some small islands Miriam commented that:

Occasionally we saw a slender column of smoke denoting the presence of human beings, probably pirates of which there were numbers about at that time. One dark night I espied a dark object resembling a boat moving very, very slowly. The Captain and the Mate saw it and examined it through the glass. [Telescope] *They could not see it distinctly but thought it was probably a boat sent to reconnoitre to see if it was possible to capture us. As our ship had two guns peeping through our port holes and we had plenty of sailors to be seen, they doubtless thought better of it. But I never slept in peace. I felt constantly in terror of them.*

Friday 1st June 1849

P.m calm. Lowered the Gig down and pulled round the ship. Observed some copper off the ship under the starboard main chain and several other sheets with nails strained. This appears very unacceptable to me for all that could possibly be got at was re -nailed in Bombay harbour. It is so far under water that it is utterly impossible to reach it until the cargo is all out and the ship heeled over.

The ship was clearly heavily loaded with something!

Monday 4th June 1849

At 6 p.m calm. At 8 p.m heavy clouds with thunder and lightning. At Midnight the wind flying about in all directions

Tuesday 5th June 1849

A.m light breezes from the sea and land alternately, trimming sail accordingly. Daylight. By the bearing of the land found that the ship had drifted to the Northward.

Noon Latitude Observation. 5. 27 Longitude chronometer 98. The lascars this morning, inclined to be troublesome.

Miriam's description of the Lascars being troublesome is considerably more dramatic!

The Lascars mutinied one morning. My husband peremptorily ordered me, nurse and Harriet immediately into our cabins and locked us in, then rushed quickly on deck. We heard a great noise and shouting and grew sick with fear. Then I heard them getting out the arms from the chest which was kept in the cuddy. By degrees the tumult subsided and we were released. It seems the Lascars tried to get possession of the fire arms. Had they not been kept in the cuddy we should have been killed. My husband and the mate, carpenter, boatswain and the doctor ran and fastened the cuddy doors and rushed onto the poop and threatened to fire on them. Finding themselves baffled they returned to duty but always after I never slept in peace, always expecting to see one of the villainous faces appearing at the cabin door, left open on account of the great heat.

It certainly was hot during this part of the voyage. The log book records temperatures well up in the 80 degrees Fahrenheit.

Alexander did not go into details and certainly did not use the word mutiny. Was Miriam exaggerating or was Alexander not wanting to dwell too much on the rioting of his crew for his employers to read. Perhaps Alexander had seen it all before and knew that his crew were trying it on and that having been defeated they would go back to work and get on with it. Managing the actual moment and quelling the riot will have required considerable fortitude and skill on the part of the Captain and his officers.

Miriam continued:

As we approached the eastern end of the straits [of Malacca] *the Islands became more numerous. We anchored for the night under the lea of one of them. Lovely, they were wooded to the water's edge and the spicy breezes coming from them were delicious.*

Meanwhile Alexander was dealing with getting through the straits.

Wednesday 6th June 1849

At 11 a.m lowered the Gig down and tried the tide by the lead. Rate of sailing 2 miles per hour. Noon. Thermometer 88. Calm. At 8 p.m looking heavy over the land with much rain and thunder and Lightning.

Friday 8th June 1849

Tried the current and found it setting to the SE. At 10 tried it again and found it setting to the NNW.

Sunday 10th June 1849

At daylight close to the Barque the Trusty which is the vessel which came up the Straits with us. Captain Barclay and a passenger came on board and remained all day.

Monday 11th June 1849

[In the middle of the Straits of Malacca.] *working all day against the wind and tide.*

P.m anchored with the small bower [anchor] *in 13 fathoms water 60 fathoms cable. Midnight more moderate with heavy rain.*

Wednesday 13th June 1849

Boarded by boats from Malacca with fish and fruit. 3 p.m tacked off at 4 tacked in and anchored with the stream to wait tide in 20 fathoms water. At 8 weighed with the wind.

Thursday 14th June 1849 [Nearly out of the straits.]

At 5 a.m calm. Dropped the stream anchor to wait tide. At 8 a light breeze with rain from the Southward. Weighed and stood to the Eastward. At 6 p.m anchored in shore to wait tide. At 9 weighed with a breeze at East. Midnight Light breezes with a cloudy appearance.

Saturday 16th June 1849

P.m wind baffling, a strong ebb tide against us. At 7.30 came too with the stream anchor in 14 fathoms water, 60 fathoms cable out to wait for daylight.

Sunday 17th June 1849

At Noon anchored well out in the Roads at Singapore in 14 fathoms water. Furled sails. This ends the passage.

The *Charlotte Jane* remained in Singapore for just two days which suggests that they probably did not off load much if any cargo.

Miriam continued:

I must not forget to say that we put in to Singapore again on our way and I again saw the fated friend who invited us to his house.

The *Charlotte Jane* sailed from Singapore on Tuesday 19th June having to keep clear of other ships one being named the *Rob Roy*!

Wednesday 27th June 1849

Alexander recorded an exciting event:

At 2 a.m Mrs Lawrence taken ill. At 4.30 she presented me with a son and heir. A fine little boy, strong and apparently a healthy child, tho' I did not expect this until after our arrival in Hong Kong. They going on very favourably.

Alexander commented that there seemed to be some inaccuracy in the Noon latitude observation and wrote:

I am therefore afraid there is some mistake as I was not present when the sun was on the meridian.

I wonder if all the crew and officers had been celebrating the birth and had not been fully concentrating in the Captain's absence!

I imagine Alexander was celebrating too. Taking his first sightings of his new little son and then perhaps introducing Harriet to her tiny baby brother. It must have been such a relief that all had gone well in the end, and been nerve wracking for Alexander when he realised the baby was coming earlier than expected. He had intended to have provided more help and comfort for Miriam.

Miriam announced the birth of her second child in the memoir in a very casual way, not ever having mentioned that she was pregnant.

She wrote:

Two days sail from Hong Kong near the Macclesfield Banks my second baby was born, Alexander Macclesfield Lawrence. Of course, such a baby "n'er was born here about nor far away." He was a bonnie boy.

Alexander recorded on

Thursday 28th June 1849

A.m fresh breezes and fine Moonlight weather, all possible sail set.

How perfect that there was a beautiful moonlit night. After the drama and effort of giving birth and having safely produced a healthy baby boy, to go with her little girl, I like to think of Miriam lying awake, probably giving thanks to God and just admiring this new little person in their lives. Of course, she may also have been feeling very sore and weepy waiting for her milk to come in, wondering how on earth she was going to cope.

Friday 29th June 1849

Fresh breeze from the Southward. Steering North. Rate of sailing 7½ miles per hour all possible sail set. Noon Latitude 18.8 North Longitude 113 52 which makes a current to the S E of 1 mile per hour. Barometer 29.82 Thermometer 86 variation 2 easterly.

P. m moderate breeze and fine all possible sail steering N ¼ E to counteract the current setting to the Eastward. Rate of sailing 6½ - 7½ miles per hour. Seeing no prospect of getting to the anchorage before dark tomorrow and one cannot be too cautious at this season on the South Coast of China. [I am not able to read the next few lines but I assume that the anchorage mentioned would have meant Hong Kong harbour, as Alexander had hoped to reach there in time for the birth. Hong Kong had been ceded to the British in the 1842 Nanjing treaty, after the first

Opium war. So, one could expect British employees to have been available for nursing and childcare work. It is something of a mystery as to where the Charlotte Jane did find anchorage.] *Midnight fine moonlight weather.*

Saturday 30ᵗʰ June 1849

A.m moderate and fine weather, all sail set. Steering N ¼ W rate of sailing 6½ – 7½ miles per hour. Daylight nothing in sight from the mast head.

Noon. Latitude 20.40 North. Longitude 114.1. The Asses ears bearing due North distant 75 miles. Barometer 29.80, Thermometer 86, variation 2 Easterly.

This is the last entry in the log book until 18th December 1849, which, is most surprising as Alexander regularly recorded coming in to harbour at the end of each passage.

The memoir recorded:

After about a fortnight's stay the orders came for us to proceed to Whampoa which is about 5 miles from Canton, to load with tea for England.

Miriam did not record where they stayed, which makes the situation even more puzzling. Perhaps Alexander had become unwell and had not been able to write his log, or for some unknown reason, decided not to record anything further? Was the cargo, possibly opium and/or onions off loaded in Hong Kong or Whampoa.? We do not even know for certain what the cargo was but we do know that the *Charlotte Jane* was definitely carrying a cargo from Bombay. I think it is the most likely time that she might have been carrying opium. Though I cannot imagine what need the Chinese would have had for any onions!

Relations between the Chinese and the British had become very strained at this time as the Nanking Treaty had forced the Chinese to keep the port of Canton, amongst others, open for trade. The Cantonese, were refusing to accept British entry into the city of Canton.

Whampoa from Danes Island, drawn by Thomas Allom, engraved by W.A.Le Petit, from
'China Illustrated 1843-1847'. (supplied by Steve Bartrick Antique prints and maps)

Trading junk, Canton, c.1870. (reproduced by permission of the Government of the HKSAR, collection
of the Hong Kong Museum of History; image P1970.22)

Chapter 7

WHAMPOA

one day up river to Whampoa

Miriam provided a fascinating description of life on board ship at anchorage in Whampoa Reach. She wrote;

We came to anchor about the centre of the stream and a mile or two from the town. At the prospect of three months 'detention' while the tea loading took place, my husband was not very pleased, and it seemed at first, rather alarming, but everything being new and fresh I was not worried and my two babies gave me plenty to think about and to do.

The climate appeared to me to be excellent, rather warm but onboard ship this is an advantage. My chief trouble was that my husband often had to go to Canton and sometimes even remain absent for two or three nights together. I felt very lonely. There was one other Captain's wife whose husband accompanied mine. We spent our lonely hours together. It would perhaps have been better if we had not, as we were both young and nervous and we used to frighten each other with stories we had heard about Captains being murdered while cruising down the Canton river, for the sake of dollars. Someone was murdered one night, soon after we left, coming from Canton with dollars. We used to sit in the darkening twilight, on the deck, listening in the silence for the sound of the oars in the rowlocks bringing our dear ones to us. Only to find it was another boat on its way to a distant ship. There would often be no sound but the melancholy cry of the corncrake on the shore or the occasional shout from a sailor in some far away vessel. At last, the well-known voices would be

*heard and they were once more, safe at home. This poor lady, who was
young and beautiful, was lost in the ship during a typhoon on her
homeward journey. The distressing thing was that her husband had
faithfully promised her mother never to take her to sea, as she had a
presentiment she would not return.*

*In the mid channel of the river in which we were anchored was a very
picturesque rock, high and covered with verdure. It had the name of
Golgotha from the number of dead bodies that were thrown there.*

*The odour on the days when the wind blew from there was not pleasant.
The setting sun used to tinge it with purple and gold, notwithstanding,
I never looked at it without disgust, as it was no uncommon thing to see a
dead body floating past with the tide or the carcasses of dead animals. As
the river water was all we had to drink, carefully filtered as it was, this
was not agreeable.*

*Harriet was very fond of looking out of the stern windows and shouting
out to the occupants of the sampans as they rowed past. She would call,
"Chin my chin chin," in her shrill voice and cry, "orangee, orangee," and
she often got them! The astonishment with which they would look, some of
them with large round, horn rimmed spectacles, was hilarious. "Hey ha
how can," they would say and stare.*

*The monotony of life was often varied. Sometimes we would see gliding
past, rowed by twelve or fourteen men, a grand flower boat in which some
grand mandarin would be taking his pleasure. These were beautifully
carved and hung with Chinese lanterns with gilt and red paper and little
flags. Then would pass like the wind a Jardine Matheson boat, long and
narrow, with a dragon prow and rowed by fifty men heaving desperately to
Canton or Hong Kong. Sometimes in the lovely cool evenings for a treat
my husband would take me for a run in a sampan some of which were kept
for the service of the ship. But this was always to me a kind of fearful joy
for they have a bamboo top to keep off the sun or rain and being shallow
they are very top heavy. Being skulled from the stern they rock to and fro
in a fearful manner. These boats were generally managed by women*

dressed in blue cotton jackets, fastened with gilt buttons, and with wide open sleeves displaying their bare sinewy arms decorated with silver bangles. Their trousers reached half way down the bare legs and they wore anklets. They were beautifully neat and clean. Their hair was shiny and smooth and decorated with white and red flowers. They managed their boats with such wonderful dexterity.

The scenery on the shore was very pretty with blue mountains in the distance and pagodas and houses with curly rooves scattered about. One or other of the ships lying at anchor was made into a church on Sundays and thither we repaired donned in our best. We always went in the ship's gig manned by six middies all in their clean white shirts and trousers looking so spick and span. A carpet was spread on deck. I used to say it was as good as one's own carriage.

A week or two passed away and my husband became impatient for the arrival of a 'chip'. A chip is a large flat vessel with enormous yellow sails on which they send down the tea from the interior. The sailors appear to bring their wives and families with them. One morning news came that a chip was in sight and appeared to be bearing down for us. At this all was activity and preparation as it fastened to the side of the ship. For about a week the noise of unloading and loading never ceased, accompanied by a babble of foreign sounds and smells of opium and garlic.

At about twelve o'clock the crew would assemble to their dinners and before each individual would be set a bowl of rice and six or seven little saucers containing various curious looking compounds with a strong smell of vinegar. Harriet and Helen would always go to watch them and they would hand up things for her to taste.

Long intervals would elapse (after unloading and loading) ere another chip came. It was rather a monotonous life. [May be the opium was unloaded at this time.]

At some point after Miriam and Alexander had arrived in Whampoa Miriam at last, received a letter from her mother.

12 Saville Row

Walworth

May 3rd 1849

My dear Miriam

We have just received your letter from Bombay and for the first time have you told us where to send to you in return. I have written once but whether it will reach you is uncertain it was addressed to Calcutta or Hong Kong. I hope you will get it. We are very glad to hear such good tidings of your health and that you are so comfortable. I am happy to say that we are all quite well, myself much improved since you left us. How often my dear girl do I think of you and long for your return which I hope will be sooner than you expect. I was pleased your little pet gets on well. How much I should like to see her. Little Evan [Miriam's youngest brother] has grown a fine little fellow very forward in mischief and very backward in talking. Little Trotty [a sister] says I am to be sure to give her love to you and that she goes to School, Alice says the same [another sister, a little older] Harriette [the sister nearest in age to Miriam] the same and she wishes you would write to her as you have written to Maria and Amelia [cousins] it has rather put her out. She has been rather poorly lately and obliged to be taken from school again. Your Uncles and aunts are still well.

The boys [Miriam's younger brothers] were at home a little while back and perfectly well and sent their love to you when I write. They very much improve.

We are very comfortable in our new house I still call it so to you. The garden is just beginning to look pleasant though the weather has been anything but favourable, such a cold spring.

Who do you think is staying with us? You and Alick will never guess I am sure. Jane Menzies poor girl she has not long lost her mother.

[The letter continues with a lot of information about the wider family which is not relevant here.]

I think I have given you all the news and is it not a great blessing that I have no bad news of ourselves to communicate and hope such will be the case till you return.

I am sorry you should imagine you were forgotten. We should have been certain to write had we known where to send to you. See how soon you hear when you let us know. I am sorry Ellen [the nurse] does not do as much as you would like you must remember that she is but young. Tell her from me that I hope she is steady and a very good girl for her poor mother's sake. Poor thing she has had plenty of trouble. Don't say so to Ellen. I don't think she will find her sister Fanny alive when she returns, for she appears to be in a rapid decline. She is married very well. I am glad she is kind to the baby that is almost everything and perhaps the heat makes her lazy.

We have been amused with your letters and all always glad when they come to assure us of your safety. You know not how much I think of you there is scarcely a night but I dream of you.

The two last letters you sent from Sydney did not arrive till about a month back, long after you had written from Hong Kong. You must have been much amused there at the ball how very strange and new everything must appear to you. Your Papa sends his kind love to you. He is looking very well and I think was never looking better. All your friends send their kindest love to you. Give ours to Alick and tell him I trust his ship will be a fortunate one. I shall look anxiously for the welcome news that you are going to start for England. You see my paper is out so must give over. Harriett desires me say she is learning music of Mrs Yatman.

Your Cousin Maria talks of writing by this packet. When you return you will see she has another added to her family. Perhaps it will be the same with you they are all very anxious to know if this is the case. I hope not. We are all quite well at present and much the same as usual longing for your return. All our love to you and kisses to baby as many as you can give her.

Your affectionate Parent.

S.H. Boddy.

We do not know when this was received but here is an important letter from Miriam letting her parents know about the birth of Alexander Macclesfield.

Whampoa

July20th 1849

My dear Mama,

I received your note when we reached Hong Kong for which short and unsatisfactory as it was many thanks.

Before I progress any further, I must tell you of an event at which I know you will be extremely surprised. I have got another little baby, a boy. He was born at sea on 27th June within three or four days from Hong Kong. I had no one but Ellen and the doctor. However, we got on very well though as you may suppose there were many inconveniences.

I did not expect it to take place until the beginning of the month when we should have been safely in China and I should have been provided with a nurse. Poor Ellen got frightened about washing the baby so I had to take it the next morning though very unfit to do so as you well know. But no ill effect arose from it and at the end of the week I was up and dressed, though very weak and now at the end of three weeks I am quite recovered and if only I could get out, should be well, but it is impossible to stir, for little Harriet, totally spoilt by Papa, does nothing but scream and run to Ellen to nurse her all day long, so that I have to nurse the baby and attend to it entirely.

I was taken ill at about 11 at night and it was all over by half past four the next morning. I have had to bear a great deal which I will tell you about when I see you again. Alick has been very kind and has done all in his power to make me comfortable. The baby is thriving. It was very small and has got an inordinately long nose. This Whampoa is a miserable place to be in for the English are not allowed to go ashore except to the town and the Lanes Island where the common sailors go. Alick says we shall most likely have to lay here three months but then there is every chance of our coming home from here. Isn't that delightful news. I think we shan't be home till Feb.

I could not write in Bombay because I was staying out all the time at one of Alick's friends.

She then writes about Bombay which I have not included as it is almost the same as her descriptions in the memoir.

The letter concludes:

Ellen was very disappointed not to get a letter she thought at least one sister would have written. You say I did not write to Maria. I am almost certain I did from China. I am writing her by this mail. I will now conclude. Give my kindest love to Papa and all my brothers and sisters and everybody else that enquires for us. I shall write again by next mail. Excuse the state of this letter for I am bothered and now goodbye.

Your truly affectionate daughter.

Miriam A Lawrence.

Miriam continued describing events at Whampoa.

One day there was a greater noise than usual mixed with weeping. With some difficulty I got the Doctor to go to see what was the matter. He had not been gone many minutes ere the noise suddenly ceased. Presently he came back and said it was a child lost overboard. I was horrified. It had gone under the ship he said, "but the mother was quite comforted when I gave her a dollar".

Some funny things happened while we were living on board. One day some painters were doing the cuddy, seeing Helen, the Nurse, with Alec in her arms they said, pointing to the child, "all same one-piece cow chile one -piece bull chile?" "Is that girl or boy?"

Another time seeing me and Helen together they said. "Heigh ya Massa Captain dis all same number one piece wife," pointing to me and then, "dis all same number two wife?" pointing to Helen.

One day they were dissatisfied with their provisions and they came aft to the Captain and said, "hammie all stinky how you like dat? Beefie all boney how you like dat? No wegecable how you like dat?"

I once employed a man to make my children's clothes and also mine. We used to talk pigeon-English. One day I gave him a piece of stuff to make a dress for Harriet, giving him as a pattern an old one with a patch on the back. To my amazement he brought it back with a patch neatly put in the new dress in exactly the same place as in the old one.

I said to him, "how can you do dat pigeon?"

He said, showing me the patch, "dis pigeon all e same dat pigeon."

I had nothing more to say. It was a point!

I like to think Miriam had a strong sense of humour as she certainly didn't seem to be cross about the patch or about Helen being wife number two!

The women did their hair very neatly though certainly the ornament they wore behind was a little like a teapot. They were artificial and I often tried to persuade the old laundress to get one for me but she always put it off.

Some gentlemen from Canton often came down for a day's shooting. They shot wild duck in the paddy fields and very nice eating they were. One day they proposed that I should be taken for a trip up one of the numerous creeks to see a little of the country. Accordingly, we started, four gentlemen, my husband and myself in the gig. The scenery on the banks was exceedingly pretty. The trees in many parts overhanging the water and lovely gardens coming down to the water's edge adorned with bridges and little pagodas and weeping willows over-hanging the water too. On our way we passed a party of ladies drinking tea in one of the gardens.

They looked pretty and smiling. They had pale complexions, jet black hair and eyebrows. Their dresses were beautifully embroidered, after staring at us for a few moments they all commenced to laugh and jumping up they scuttled off as fast as their poor little feet would let them.

We continued our journey and in a little time came to a small village on the banks of the creek where some fete was in progress. Seeing no one about Mr W thought we might land and look about us. We went into a large square tent at the top of which were several gigantic figures dressed in splendid embroidered silk robes like the mandarins. The whole hall was ornamented with red and gold and Chinese characters in black.

Down the centre was a long table on which was set out many curious things but we had not time to look at them for suddenly we heard a noise of running feet and Mr W called out to us, "run, run" and we did run with numbers of Chinese after us. We were only just in time for they surrounded me and tried to carry me off but the gentlemen used their sticks pretty freely and I was hustled quickly into the boat safely. I was much frightened. Only a short time before some Chinamen had imprisoned an English lady, a Captain's wife, and carried her about in a cage for some days as a show. I believe she was sent for by Queen Victoria, afterwards, to tell of her adventures. After this adventure we rowed home to the ship and thought we had better not land again.

A short time before this my husband, Harriet and I had gone ashore for a walk. We went through a small wood in which we saw a small temple beneath a large tree. We went inside and found an altar on which were placed ornaments and joss sticks and yellow and red paper. It was exactly similar to an altar to the Virgin Mary. We went on and came to a small village which we thought of entering but the children threw stones at us calling out, "fanque fo io fanqui fo! Foreign devils look at the foreign devil's wife." So, we thought we had better beat a retreat. In those days an English lady was scarcely ever seen in China.

China is a pretty country at least around Whampoa and Canton. If anyone wants to see what it is like he need only look at an old-fashioned willow patterned plate, the same trees, same little bridges, pagodas and curly roofed houses.

I had another adventure which to this day I never think of without horror. The Doctor who had been very ill thought it would do us all good to go ashore and proposed we should take a boat, Helen, Harriet, myself, the baby and the Doctor. My husband being away on business. So, we went on a ship's boat manned by our own sailors and after rather a long row, landed near some paddy fields. The paddy or rice grows in water and each field is separated from each other by narrow paths just wide enough to walk upon. The paddy, look like very green grass. It was pleasant enough at first but when we had been walking about an hour it became just a little wearisome. The boat had been told to meet us just a little way further along the shore. Just when we were getting tired out, we came near to the village at the waterside where we were to meet the boat. To my horror I found that the only way to get to that village, was over a narrow plank just wide enough for one person at a time. This plank was put over a very wide and apparently deep open cesspool from which exuded a stench enough to knock one down. There was no protection to keep one from falling if one's foot slipped. My heart sank within me. I felt I could not cross it and that I should be sure to fall. I turned dizzy and sick at the thought of crossing it and I did not know what to do.

The doctor did his best to cheer me up but the idea of falling into that dreadful slough completely did for me and I trembled all over. We could not go back as the boat was to wait for us there. Helen, Harriet and the baby got safely over. After some time, the doctor proposed that he should go before me and that I should take hold of his stick. Eventually I screwed up sufficient courage and so step by step, holding the doctor's stick, with many pauses and heart searching, I at last succeeded in crossing, but I did not recover from the horror for a long time and to this day I cannot go over a plank. The people all ran out to look at us as we walked through the village and the children accompanied us to the boat and stroked Harriet's cheeks and looked at their fingers to see if the whiteness came off. How grateful I was when we reached our boat and were safely on our way to our ship. It was a very foolish excursion and one my husband would not have allowed, had he been on board but he was at Canton at the time.

I do wonder whether the Doctor held his stick out behind him for Miriam to grasp or perhaps went shuffling sideways. I can't think he walked backwards!

Alexander wrote a belated letter to his father-in-law.

October 26th 1849

My dear Doctor,

It is now a long time since I wrote to you but I believe Minnie has written every mail. Really, I have been so much annoyed lately that I have not been in the humour to write to anyone except in business. I expected by this time to have been in England but so it is. We are still here and I am glad to say that both Minnie and myself and children are tolerably well. The young things are teething and consequently a little cross. There are two or three ladies amongst the ships in Whampoa reach otherwise it would be very dull for Minnie.

I have not been treated well by our hosts here otherwise the 'Charlotte Jane' ought to have been loaded long ago. We have only two hundred tins? of tea on board and when I shall get away it is almost impossible for me to say. Sometime before the new year, I hope. There are an immense number of ships here and freights are consequently low. £3.10 which will not cover expenses on the round.

Minnie has got some small presents for the children and I shall get some Manilla for you if possible before I leave. We observe by the papers that the cholera is bad in London. We hope that you all have escaped. There has been a good many changes amongst our connections since we left especially in the Menzies family. I low is Bill Smith getting on poor fellow? I fear it is up hill with him, the same as myself at present but things will mend.

I do not know what effect the new navigation law being repealed will have, but if there is anything like fair play Englishmen will compete with any nation. I was glad to hear some time ago from George Thomson that Danse was getting on well in Buenos Ayres. I hope this is really the case and that in a short time he will be able to return to England with a competency.

I long to be amongst you again in Walworth. Minnie will finish this letter with something in her manner, so that I conclude with love to Mrs Boddy, yourself and the children who will be much altered before we see them. Believe me Sir

Yours affectionately

Alexander Lawrence.

[The Navigation Act 1849 aimed to promote 'free trade' initiatives and repealed many protectionist import and export duties on manufactured goods.]

Miriam unwillingly added to Alexander's letter.

My dear Mama,

Alick has said I am to write, otherwise I don't think I should have written this mail, for I am not well this evening and I have nothing to say. We are you see in the same abominable place. I am so sick of it. I am miserable. At least I should be so if I had not one or two ladies to keep me in company. They are very pleasant, one or two others not so good themselves but you can afford to laugh at them for nothing and treat them with the contempt they deserve. The children are awfully cross with their teeth. Little Harriet is a second Aleck boohooing terribly if she is not allowed to do just as she pleases. My little boy 'Aleck the less' is a very fine child. I am very proud of him. I wish you could see him he is just beginning to know one. He is now four months old. This is the unhealthy season for agues and fevers and I am afraid I have got a touch. I know I had last night but I must hope it will soon take its departure. I feel very queer today. I don't know what I shall do with the children if I get ill. It is a horrid thing that cold feeling I have and then as if you are in a fire, but hope for the best. Ellen is very well and shouts the only thing she complains of, is that pimples are coming in her face, a very sound ailment! She sends her love and wishes she were at home again. I must now bid you all farewell. I am sure you will excuse my not doing a long letter. If you don't get one next mail, you may conclude we are on our way home to dear old England which I hope will be.

What a tough time they all seemed to be having stuck at Whampoa. The memoir continued with further descriptions of events in Whampoa Reach.

One night we saw on the vessel opposite to where our ship was lying, (a tongue of land divided the two reaches) a bright light as if something was on fire. While we were speculating what it could be, a boat came alongside bringing news that pirates had attacked and were burning a large vessel and begging for all who could to go to their assistance. The burning went on all night and we heard next morning that some of the crew were near death, some murdered and some escaped. The poor captain and the mate had gone over the stern and saved themselves by hanging on some chains all night, half in the water. They were rescued next day by those who went to help, more dead than alive. I believe the pirates got clean off. This event made me very unhappy as there appeared no reason why we should not suffer in like manner.

One afternoon we had just finished tea when a note was put in my hand from the wife of a captain of a nearby ship, saying she would be greatly obliged if Mrs Lawrence would go to see her as she was in trouble and would be glad of some advice. After some consideration my husband consented to my going and that he would accompany me. So, calling a sampan we started. After a rather long row we arrived at the ship and I was ushered into the cabin where was seated an elderly lady attended by a Hindoo girl busily engaged in fanning her mistress with a huge fan of peacock feathers. The lady expressed her gratitude for my granting her request and said had she known I was so young she would not have sent for me. The truth was, she said a most unpleasant thing had happened. She had brought with her as an attendant, a young English girl and that morning she had been found dead in her bed. She feared foul play and suspected the steward, but had no evidence and hoped for some advice. Of course, inexperienced as I was, I could give none. There was no possibility of an inquest and there seemed no way of solving the mystery. After a little time, talking we thought we had better go as it was useless involving ourselves up in the affair but I have often thought about that poor young

*girl dying there far away from home and friends, perhaps murdered.
We heard no more about it and the ship sailed away shortly afterwards.
The poor lady seemed in great distress.*

*Varied by these events and the arrival of Chips of tea which always caused
great excitement, three months passed away, when one day a note arrived
from Mrs Maclean, inviting me and my babies to stay at Canton. My
delight was unbounded to think I was to set foot in that mysterious city,
where few Europeans were allowed to enter. There was only one street that
any foreigner might go. So, we went up the river in a ship's boat
sometimes rowing sometimes sailing, passing through crowds of junks and
duly arrived at a fine house. There were several houses close together
inhabited by different merchants. The house was very spacious and
substantial with deep verandas paved with black and white marble,
protected from the sun by green blinds or jalouses (shutters made with a
row of slats to keep out rain and sun). The verandas were furnished with
cane lounging chairs and tables with books and flowers, a pleasant place
for a hot day with the sea breezes blowing gently through the jalouses.
There were marble baths and every luxury. I was much struck by the
clever waiting at table of the Chinese 'boys' as the attendants were called,
some grey haired! One thing to complain of was that being in full dress the
pigtail was allowed to hang down and with the rapidity of their
movements this would swing round threatening to whisk the glasses off the
table and occasionally coming in unpleasant proximity to one's face.*

*An excursion into the city itself was arranged for my benefit. So, one fine
morning Harriet, nurse, baby and I were put into a sedan chair carried by
four coolies who grunted in a most alarming way as they rolled along with
their burden. They always do so. There was only one street that we were
allowed to enter and that not a very long one. Into this we were carried. It
was full of coolies dressed only in a linen cloth, hurrying along carrying
their burdens in their own peculiar fashion, at each end of a bamboo slung
over the shoulders. They were dressed only in a linen cloth round their
loins. There were a few better dressed. Some few Englishmen were there.
All the shops had bamboo shutters with gilt or black painted on them.
They had curly roofs. The dust, the smells and the crowds were not
agreeable. As soon as it was perceived that English women were in the*

sedan chair crowds of coolies ran after us and when we came to the curio shop and the chair was put down for us to alight, they pressed round pushing their faces close to ours and grinning and shouting in a most unpleasant manner. The gentleman with us hustled them back and us into the shop as quickly as possible, and as they began to crowd in after us, he put up his shutters and barricaded his door. The shop was full of beautiful things. We bought tables and vases which I brought home with us. Then, followed by our crowd we were taken back to Mrs Maclean's house. Another day we were taken to see Howqua's Garden. Howqua was a rich merchant who kindly allowed people to inspect his lovely garden and house.

He was famous for being thought to be the richest man on earth. He had died in 1843 and it is possible that when Miriam went there the garden may have begun to deteriorate although there is some evidence that visitors continued to visit even into the 1900's to take photographs.

Miriam wrote:

The garden was very pretty and quaint with small bridges over artificial streams, waterfalls, curious rocks on which were perched pagodas and little curly roofed houses with walls with oval openings which seemed to have a beautifying effect on the landscape seen through them. Then there was the dwarf garden in which there were miniature trees of all species quite perfect but bearing all the marks of extreme age, gnarled mossy trunks and thin leaved. None of them were more than a yard high. We also saw Howqua's house. The most I remember about it was that it had no glass windows only semi-transparent paper on which were painted birds and chrysanthemums In the walls were oval openings and ornamental balconies.

Later Miriam was taken to a rather different place of interest.

Then we went to see a Soy manufacturer. There were immense vats full of dark coloured liquid, in the open air, on the top of which floated something very like cockroaches and I believe they were. I will tell you why. All the time we lay in Whampoa reach, an old Chinaman used to come every morning to fetch away a number of cockroach traps he laid over night.

They were always full of the nasty things. I was told that every ship had a cockroach catcher. No Chinaman will do anything unless he is to make money and this old fellow begged us as a favour to be allowed to take away the creatures so they must make some money out of them.

I gather cockroaches were also in such demand because they were used as fishing bait and for medicinal purposes.

Miriam continued:

The atmosphere of Canton was peculiar. Indeed, the whole of the part of China in which I was, seemed full of the scent of Joss stick, which they burn before their gods and which is made of asses dung mixed with garlic. Indeed, everything appeared to me to taste of garlic even the oranges of which there are a great variety. The finest being the Coolie.

It was curious to see the numbers of kites in the shapes of owls and dragons flying over the city. The Chinese are great at kite flying and also at shuttlecock which they play with their feet. Our visit was brought to an end and we returned to our ship. I was glad to get back. True there were no marble baths and our berths were small but it was home.

Miriam seems to have really enjoyed her stay in Canton and been very interested in everything she had seen in the different places she had visited.

She wrote:

One day I was asked by way of a little change from the usual monotony, to inspect some Indian worked muslin dresses that had been brought from Bombay by a captain's wife on board her husbands' ship. The cabins were spacious and were arranged like a beautiful London drawing room with china vases, muslin hangings and Indian work of all varieties, everything suggestive of life at sea being carefully hidden. I bought a few things. The articles however, that she had to dispose of were of no value, being but bad specimens of the lovely Indian work. I was told that many Captain's wives made a good deal of money in this way, selling things to the mates and captain's wives from other ships, who would go and buy things to take home, being of course no judge of the value and so paying a great deal for little worth.

Finally, after spending almost six months in Whampoa Miriam wrote:

By this time the old ship was fairly full and the Captain was thinking of turning his face homeward. Good news for me for our stock of wearing apparel was nearly exhausted having been nearly two years travelling about, and I was getting homesick.

In November Miriam wrote a letter to her mother.

The Charlotte Jane

Whampoa Reach

November 6th 1849

My dear Mama and Papa

At last, I am able to send home the welcome news I am sure, to you that we are coming home to old England once more. By the time you get this we shall, I trust be a good part of our way home. I am delighted at the idea of it though there is many a long weary mile to go over, many dangers to pass through and many a dreary hour. I feel as if I am almost home and often, find myself anticipating the joyful meeting with you all.

It has been a dreary enough time here. I am sure since I last wrote to you, I have had the ague, however I only had two fits and soon recovered. Alick has also had it but is better now though not well, at which I am not at all surprised for the poor fellow is dreadfully worried and irritated for this has been a sad boring voyage, and the long delay before being loaded.

We are now only half loaded but hope to get away the first week in next month and shall not be here another minute. So, this is the last you will hear of us until we get to London. I hope we shall find you all well. The cholera makes me tremble for you all. By this last mail we hear that it is very bad in London but I hope you will have escaped it. I dare say we shall find every one of you all very much changed as you will find us. We shall each of us be two years older. Alick looks a little older, I think. Ellen from a girl is becoming a young woman and a little improved in her looks, certainly in her own opinions. It will be a load off my mind to have her home. So far no one but those who have tried and experienced it can have any idea of the charge and trouble of a European servant girl out in these countries. It spoils them to bring them out here. I will never do it again. I shall come home with two babies instead of one and of course I can't know whether I look older but I do think I am probably more matronly looking. Little Harriet is a fat chubby little creature. I send you a piece of her hair it is so pretty. My little boy is growing a really beautiful little fellow he is very fair and has a -----colour, dark hair and eyebrows, a well-formed nose, not an ambitious one, but one that seeks the ground, a gay pretty mouth like little Barnard's [one of Miriam's brothers] and eyes as blue as the sea, they look sometimes to me like the ocean asleep in the evening and long black eyelashes. Now don't laugh at all this about my boy, you will see I am not partial! I call him, my little seabird, he can truly say by and bye he was cradled in the deep. I think all this is very likely, now I think of it, to annoy Papa as I know how averse he can be to anything sentimental. However, he must excuse it in this letter as it is the last, I shall trouble you with for some time. There is a ship here going to Buenos Ayres I am going to write to my Aunt Dixon by it and Alick intends doing the same to my dear Uncle George.

We have no passengers from here for which I am very sorry. I dare say it will be very dull. So long a passage from December to the end of March or the commencement of April. I sincerely hope we shall get safe home. I get very dull at sea and frightened. I can't sleep and awaken at the least noise. Somehow a sort of mistrust seems to get one when a squall is coming and company drives away all thoughts a great deal; but perhaps it is as well that we have no passengers for the ladies here are an absurd set. They think so much of themselves and many do not consider a Captain's wife good enough to associate with, but I make it a rule to treat them as haughtily as they do me, for I am better than any out here just now.

I don't think I have any more to say except bid you all a merry Christmas and a Happy New Year. Think of us in those days when we shall be far away on the dark blue ocean perhaps in a storm. We will think of you all and drink your health's and now my dear parents and very dear brothers and sisters and all, farewell. It may be that we are not to meet again in this world. We may find our graves in the bottom of the great deep. If it is so ordained God grant that we may all meet in Heaven never to separate. We have many dangers to pass through but I hope and trust that we shall yet be allowed to meet you all again but we know that is uncertain. In the meantime, goodbye and God bless you all. Alick sends his fondest love to you my dear Papa and my dear Mama in which I most heartily join. Give my kind love to all our friends and my dear brothers and sisters and ever believe me my dear parents, I am

Your truly affectionate daughter Miriam Lawrence.

Ellen is writing something on a small piece of paper. Pray excuse this untidy and badly written letter but this is with shocking paper and there is no other to be got here.

So, the carefree young woman who set off on this voyage, afraid of nothing, having complete faith in her husband, had changed into a most loving and devoted mother, more worried and anxious, and fully aware of all the possible dangers at sea, and longing for home. By now preparations for departure began to be made for the long voyage home. Neither the log book nor the memoir record what these were. But there must have been much to do. Some new sailors would need to be recruited and fresh water and food supplies taken on board as well as making sure the ship was in good shape. Miriam and Alexander and the family stayed their last few days in Canton before joining the *Charlotte Jane*.

Miriam explained;

Mrs M, the agent's wife was away from home but the gentleman at the head of affairs invited us to spend the last two or three days at Canton. The Captain being busy we remained all the time in the house with the exception of two or three rows on the river Tigris [the estuary of the Pearl River.] Our rooms were at the back of the house past which ran one of numerous small creeks going down to the river. I could hardly sleep at night for the cries of the children, who kept a low moaning sound all night. Mr G said it was because their feet were bound.

Another dreadful noise that went on continuously was made by the knocking together of bamboo sticks by the watchmen. This was to let people know that they were awake and watching.

At last, the time came for us to quit this queer celestial land. In order that we might travel comfortably a flower boat with large airy cabins and cushioned seats, rowed by eight Chinamen was engaged to convey us to the ship. I was charmed at the delight of the beautiful boat and anticipated a pleasant journey. We were delayed starting and evening was coming on when at last we took our departure. We had been rowed for about an hour when the men suddenly refused to go any further paying no heed to my husband's remonstrations. Here was a fix. The rascals had already been paid.

No other boat was to be got now, the open sea far away from Canton and the Charlotte Jane not in sight. The men said they would row us back but said it was too late to go further away from Canton. The captain was in despair and at his wits end, it was nearly dark and the babies were hungry and tired and crying. Several fishing boats were in sight and my husband hailed one and after some bargaining the fisherman consented to take us to the ship. So, in the darkness and in mid ocean I and my babies and bundles and nurse were somehow transferred from the large roomy cushioned boat to the stuffy little cabin of the fishing vessel which however was beautifully clean. We were taken down to the main cabin where we found the wife and two children who sat and stared at us in consternation. In one corner of this tiny place was what appeared to be a small altar on which was the figure of a woman very like the Virgin Mary, adorned with flowers and gilt paper and a joss or incense stick burning before it. I suppose it was the Fisherman's Goddess. We sailed on for some time with no sign of the ship. Fortunately, the sea was not rough. I was terribly tired and the poor babies were restless, tired, cold and hungry. My husband was in a great state of anxiety fearing the ship was too far out for us to get to her. Certainly, things did look bleak, wife and children on board a small boat in the open sea, far from land, no provisions and the night dark and lowering. I felt I was, falling into a doze in spite of my anxiety, when I heard his cheery voice saying he saw her lights and in a short time we were alongside the Charlotte Jane and quickly hoisted on board.

Miriam does not mention how the hoisting was achieved in the dark, what with masses of skirt to manage, exhaustion and two weary children.

How cosy the cuddy looked and how snug our little cots and how thankfully I settled that night once more, safe in our floating home.

The Canton Factories along the Pearl River in southwestern Canton where European merchants lived and traded under strict conditions; the British establishment is located behind the church.
(courtesy of the Peabody Essex Museum of Salem)

Canton, mid 19th century.

Tsiang-Lan-Kiai Street, Canton, c.1870. (courtesy Hulton Archive of Getty Images)

A Street in Canton, drawn by Thomas Allom, engraved by W.H.Capade, from
'China Illustrated 1843-1847' (supplied by Steve Bartrick Antique prints and maps)

Cap-Vender's Shop, Canton, drawn by Thomas Allom, engraved by W.Floyd, from
'China Illustrated 1843-1847'. (supplied by Steve Bartrick Antique prints and maps)

House of a Chinese Merchant, near Canton, drawn by Thomas Allom, engraved by W.H.Capade,
from 'China Illustrated 1843-1847' (supplied by Steve Bartrick)

Howqua's Garden circa 1836, gouache on paper, studio of Guan Lianchang, also known as Tingqua
(Chinese, active 1830-1879). (courtesy of the Peabody Essex Museum of Salem; image E83532.16,
Augustine Heard Collection)

Natives of Cochin-China playing at Shittlecock with their Feet, W. Alexander del. S.Landseer & S.Shirt sculp. (courtesy Government Art Collection; image GAC16970)

Preparing tea for export, c.1870 (courtesy Hulton Deutsch Collection, Getty Images)

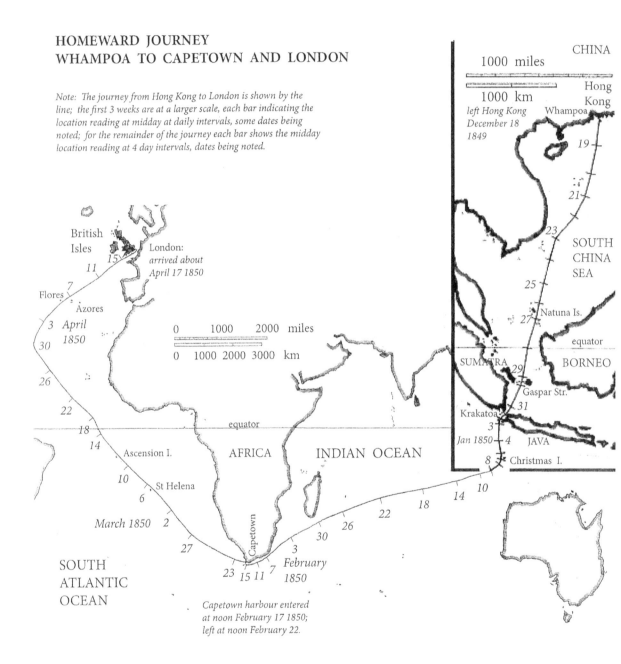

HOMEWARD JOURNEY
WHAMPOA TO CAPETOWN AND LONDON

Note: The journey from Hong Kong to London is shown by the line; the first 3 weeks are at a larger scale, each bar indicating the location reading at midday at daily intervals, some dates being noted; for the remainder of the journey each bar shows the midday location reading at 4 day intervals, dates being noted.

CHINA

1000 miles

Hong Kong

1000 km

left Hong Kong December 18 1849

Whampoa

19

21

23

SOUTH CHINA SEA

25

27 Natuna Is.

equator

SUMATRA   29   BORNEO

Gaspar Str.

31

Krakatoa

3

Jan 1850 — 4   JAVA

8 Christmas I.

British Isles

15

11

London:
arrived about April 17 1850

7

Flores

Azores

3 *April 1850*

30

26

22

18   equator

14

Ascension I.   AFRICA   INDIAN OCEAN

10

St Helena

6

March 1850   2

27

Capetown

23 15 11 7   3 *February 1850*

30

26

22

18

14   10

10

SOUTH ATLANTIC OCEAN

Capetown harbour entered at noon February 17 1850; left at noon February 22.

0   1000   2000 miles

0   1000 2000 3000 km

Chapter 8

FROM WHAMPOA TO CAPE TOWN

Sixty-One days at sea

Having safely arrived back in *the Charlotte Jane after* the adventure in the fishing boat, Miriam wrote:

The next day it came on to blow heavily, nearly a hurricane accompanied by the most tremendous show of lightning and thunder I have ever seen. Balls of coloured fire and forked lightning seemed to be falling in all directions. The electric fluid seemed to be all over the ship and around us, it was awful and it blew so hard one could not stand up. The sky was like ink. Fortunate it was for us that we were at anchor and in a comparatively sheltered place.

I wonder if the flower boat rowers who refused to go out to sea any further had an inkling that this storm was imminent, and I worry that the little fishing vessel that so gallantly stepped in to help may have got caught by it.

The next day fine weather prevailed and we bade a long farewell to the flowery land and set sail for the Cape of Good Hope.

I am surprised Miriam was not thanking God to be leaving China at last but something about the beauty of the place and people seems to have touched her despite all the difficulties, discomforts and horrors they encountered during their time in Whampoa. 40 years distance might have helped!

The *Charlotte Jane* picked up the Lawrence family out at sea and then proceeded on to Hong Kong harbour, where they probably stayed for a few days making final preparations before setting sail for Cape Town.

Miriam wrote:

We only remained here [Hong Kong] a short time and I only went ashore to see a friend once. I lived on the ship.

Alexander wrote in the log book:

18th December 1849 Tuesday.

Crew more or less inebriated especially those who shipped at Hong Kong. [Perhaps they were high on opium or some such substance.]

At 10 a.m weighed and made sail out of Hong Kong harbour, at 4 p.m abreast of the Asses ears from which I take my departure.

Wednesday 19th December 1849

Crew still queer.

Sunday 23rd December 1849

At 10.30 a.m squally with heavy rain unable to have divine service.

Probably because the hold was so full of tea and because of the rain.

Tuesday 25th December 1849 CHRISTMAS DAY

Midnight fine Moonlight.

Once again there is no mention of Christmas in the log or the memoir, but I imagine they all drank everyone's health and perhaps enjoyed the beautiful moonlight.

Saturday 29ᵗʰ December 1849

Breeze increasing and squally at 10 a.m very squally. Noon very strong breeze after the squall. Carrying on to make Gasper Island before dark. At 7.30 p.m anchored in 13 fathoms of water under the S.E. part of Gasper Island to wait for daylight. Midnight moderate with rain.

Miriam wrote about this part of the journey when they were on their way to Bombay. I have placed it here so it fits with the log book.

I have another adventure to tell you about. At the Java end, near the Straits of Malacca, about 5 miles from the shore are two islands called the Brothers. To go between these islands instead of round them saves a good deal of time. After consulting together, the mate and my husband decided that the wind being fair they would go between the islands but scarcely had we sailed a mile or two and got fully into the narrow channel the wind clipped round. The sky became overcast and it came on to blow furiously. The whole day did we tack and tack every hour, I think, making scarcely any progress and wearing out the sailors. My husband was nearly despairing and the men worn out. There was no anchorage. As a last resort my husband decided to run for a very small bay to try for anchorage, though the chances were, I heard that there was none. In which case we would have gone on the rocks and perhaps become prey of pirates of which there was no lack at that time. Suddenly a slant of wind came most providentially and took us clear out of the passage in half an hour.

Alexander wrote about this in the log.

Sunday 30ᵗʰ December 1849

Squally from N.W. At 7 a.m weighed and made sail through Gasper Straits. At noon passed through the straits entrance point. Squally with heavy rain and an increasing breeze. Steering to make the land inside the Brothers. Midnight same weather.

Monday 31st December 1849

Fresh breeze and fine at 3.30 a.m passed between a ship and Barque at anchor which rather surprised me having plenty of time till daylight for the Brothers. At daylight got into 5-7 fathoms of water. Kept off South for the Brothers. At noon passed inside of the Brothers a French ship in company named the Cesar Nicholas. At 3 p.m very squally working between St Nicholas point and the Sumatra shore.

Tuesday 1st January 1849 Actually 1850!

Moderate and fine. At daylight tacked from the middle of the straits wind at N.W. Lying up for the passage between the Storm rock and Zutphen Island. At 10 was boarded by several of the boats from Anger and Sumatra shore. At 5 p.m passed the Storm rock with a strong westerly current but which changes at 6 o'clock made a tack to the Northward, at 9 tacked to the S.W. Lying well up for Cracatoe Island. Midnight a squally appearance. [This was before Krakatoa Island erupted.]

Wednesday 2nd January 1849 [Still!]

A.m at 2 violent squalls from the Westward with heavy rain. Split Jib, flying jib and fore top gall sail, endeavouring to carry on to pass through Princes straights. Ship during the squalls turned over on her broadside had to lower the topsails down. Noon entering Princes straights, pumps attended to as much as possible. P.m wind baffling under the land. At 3.30 p.m got a breeze from the Southward but very baffling. Working out of the straight with violent squalls ship thrown over. At 5.30 while just rounding the point the wind failed leaving us in anything but a pleasant situation. Managed to get her round and cleared the rocks -------to anchorage. A dirty squally night and only room between the rocks on each side of the straights. The seamen from previous intoxication at Hong Kong unable to work the ship properly and I fear that during this time the pumps were not properly attended to. At 11.30 tacked and the breeze increasing a little, made an attempt to stand out. cleared everything which eased *my mind. This being my third night without sleep as soon as the head of Java was 6 miles off. I turned in, still a very squally appearance.*

This must have been a marathon three nights and made the more worrying as Alexander was not very confident in all the members of his crew. I wonder if this route through the Brothers did save time as Miriam explained had been the plan. It is interesting that Miriam did not remember the boat being thrown over twice nor that they lost some sails. 40 years after the event it is amazing how much she did recall. She may have kept letters and diaries to help her which have since been lost.

She certainly remembered the sudden welcome wind that puffed the *Charlotte Jane* most fortuitously through the straits between Princes Island and the Head of Java.

Alexander recorded:

Saturday 5th January 1849

Daylight the vessels in sight gained on us during the night which does not a little annoy me showing some inattention on the part of the officers to our sails during the night.

During the next three days the rate of sailing was very slow ranging from 1 mile per hour up to 2½ miles per hour which will have been tiresome for everyone and especially frustrating for Alexander who liked hurrying along. On the fourth day the wind increased and the rate of sailing rose to between 6 and 7 miles per hour. They spotted several other ships during these days and exchanged colours with one or two.

Thursday 17 January 1849 [Corrected to 1850.]

Sunday 20th January 1850

Midnight Squally and the people not steering well.

Monday 21st January 1850

Midnight. Fine weather. The upper send over the moon.

[When a ship is pitching up and down and the moon full, on the up rise it appears as if the ship is above the moon! This sounds amazing to see].

Sunday 22nd January 1850

P.m brisk trade wind and fine all possible sail set to advantage. Clear moonlight some light and high send coming over the moon from the Northward As the weather keeps pretty cool and the barometer high, I do not anticipate any change. Midnight fine weather.

Wednesday 30th January 1850

Bellenham, Ordinary seaman refused duty and was put in irons. At 10 a.m called the officers and the doctor into the cabin and tried this seaman. Found him guilty and ordered him to be sent to grease the.... (I am not able to read this word) each Saturday which is the usual time for doing that duty until the order is countermanded.

This sounds to be quite a lenient punishment, though I may not understand how horrible a job it might be or for how long he might have to go on doing it! I wonder if he was one of the seamen who had been inebriated.

Monday 4th February 1950

P.m heavy head sea retarding our progress. Midnight same weather.

Wednesday 6th February 1850

Midnight moderate with a very unsettled appearance. Sounded in 53 fathoms, calm. Sand with pieces of shell.

Thursday 7th February 1850

A.m nearly calm with a heavy head sea from the westward. Ship pitching and knocking about a great deal.

It sounds very wild. I wonder if Miriam and others were suffering with sea sickness.

Miriam wrote in her memoir;

Nothing much happened on our way to the Cape of Good Hope except another mutiny which broke out among the seamen. I do not know why but one morning a seaman after a great deal of noise, rushed up onto the poop and attacked my husband who, then, had the strength of two men and who took him by the collar and dashed him over the poop onto the deck. A number of other sailors began to swear and bawl. My husband ordered me downstairs and then he rushed to the arms chest and taking a cutlass drew a line amidships with it on the deck and stood there threatening to cut the first seaman down who passed it. I was looking out of the cuddy windows and saw all this. Some of the men were stripped to the waist and looked very terrible to me as they were rampaging about but none dared to cross the line. By and bye the ringleaders were found out and handcuffed and confined. I heard one being brought down to the cuddy swearing and straining. The doctor said to him, "Hush my lad, don't you know there are ladies here?" Whereupon the poor fellow said, "Bless their little hearts I would not hurt them for the world" and though he was in the next cabin to me I never heard a single sound more. They were taken on shore at Cape Town and tried and duly punished but very lightly.

Here is Alexander's record of this event.

Sunday 10th February 1850

A.m strong breezes. At 4 Hove ship in shore. Split the main sail. At 6 ordered the mainsail to be unbent for the purpose of being repaired, not having a spare one and tho' Sunday I very reluctantly ordered the seamen along with the sail maker to repair it, when the seamen Bates and Robinson came aft and said they thought it not right to repair sails on Sunday and after a good deal of insolence from Bates, saying that the mainsail ought to have been unbent long ago and that the ship ought to have another main sail and that repairing sails was not according to the scriptures; they went to work: but Bates, being evidently dissatisfied and only going thro' the form I told him to go forward. That I did not want anyone to work who was so dissatisfied and he went forward. After some

*consideration I thought this such a gross case of misconduct that I
deemed it necessary to put a stop to it.*

Alexander had had a couple of hours to think and was perhaps
hoping to regain authority and be seen to take full control of the situation,
when he again spoke to Bates in what sounded like, a rather sarcastic
tone.

*At 2 p.m about to tack ship when I asked Bates if he thought it
necessary to Tack ship as he thought the mainsail ought to have
been unbent long ago and that the ship ought to have two mainsails.
He became very insolent and abusive and called me a B---- f--- liar.
I was going up to calm him when the mate rushed at him and he
commenced striking right and left and I took me several blows on
the face. Then Leese, Seaman collared the Chief mate saying he
could not stand and see two to one. A general scuffle ensued. Bates
was secured and put in irons and put into one of the water closets in
the Cuddy. It must be understood that this water closet has not
been used it being full of tea since leaving China. As soon as quiet
was restored called Leese aft and read the law to him that he had
been guilty of mutiny but he said that he knew the laws as well
as I did from the books.*

Clearly, violence had occurred and Alexander had been hit on the face by
one of his crew, a clear case of insubordination. Fortunately, no serious
injuries were recorded

Miriam was uncertain in her own mind as to what actually happened as
she wrote two versions of this event. In this one, she described having
witnessed it from on deck and then from the cuddy window. In the other
she wrote that after seeing Alexander being hit, she was sent below and
saw nothing further. Once again, with the grandchildren in mind I have
chosen the more dramatic version as it is like a film. I can imagine the
children acting out being the Captain drawing the line on the deck, with
his cutlass and no one daring to disobey their grandfather who had the
strength of two men, at that time!

I hope Bates really did say, "Bless their little hearts I would not hurt them for the world," as he was pushed down into the cuddy, as it provides an indication of the respect, he and perhaps several of the crew felt for Miriam and Helen and the children.

The next day Alexander wrote:

Monday 11th February 1850

At 2 a.m attempted to reef the fore top sail with the watch as had been done before frequently but they could not or rather would not hoist the sail up. Called the hands out to shorten sail and found them all slack in getting the sail reefed.

Alexander must have been annoyed and anxious at the laxity of the crew. But he seems to have managed the situation as they continued on the voyage without further problems of this sort.

When they had nearly reached South Africa Miriam commented:

Just before getting into the Cape we experienced a SE wind or 'South Easter'. It blows more vertically. I went on deck to see the gale. What a terrible and yet lovely sight. The sun was shining brightly. The wind was so high that it blew the sea to a fine spray so as to have the effect of a haze. The huge waves like mountains or huge green dragons tipped with foam came thundering towards us threatening to overwhelm our puny ship. Just when they appeared to be about to engulf us, we would find ourselves on the top of one looking down on to a green watery chasm. I could not stay long it looked so fearful.

Alexander wrote:

Thursday 14th February 1850

Midnight breeze increasing from the S.E.

Friday 15th February 1850

Strong breezes. Rate of sailing 9 miles per hour, afraid to run into anchorage it blowing so strong from the S.E. Waiting for the gale to abate. Midnight less wind.

Saturday 16th February 1850

A.m strong breezes from S E. At 8 calm. 10. Thick weather and continued till noon. No observation. Cleared up at 1 p.m when Table summit distant 20 miles. Calm all afternoon. At 6 quite thick at 8 a breeze from the N.W. Stood in shore quite thick at 11 tacked ship stood to the N.W.

Sunday 17th February 1850

At 2 a.m tacked ship stood in E.N.E. At daylight fetched in to windward of Hind Bay. At Noon anchored in Table Bay in 5 fathoms water and 10 cables out. Went on shore and went out to Mr Billings.

In 2012 Hal and I went to Cape Town. I tried to find out what happened to Bates and Robinson but without success. However, I did manage to see a record of the *Charlotte Jane's* arrival in Table Bay and her departure. For some reason this gave me a great sense of achievement which I thought surprising as I already had that information from the log!

Miriam wrote:

Table Bay is very lovely with Table Mountain and Cape Town nestling at its foot. Before the South Easter comes to blow, a heavy white cloud rolls over the top which is as flat as a table. The inhabitants call it the table cloth. The climate was delicious. We were there in the grape season. We were invited to stay at a Mr Billings house some distance from the town. He had a lovely house and a vinery half a mile in length. The vines bearing grapes of every description were mainly over a trellis and the splendid bunches hung down within reach of one's hand. We made an excursion to Wineberg, where the manufacture of the delicious Cape liqueur and wine was made. We saw Mr and Mrs Chloet the proprietors and spent some time walking about the pretty grounds.

Hal and I visited the same vineyard. We felt we were really treading in the same shoes as Miriam and Alexander.

Miriam continued:

We only remained a week at the Cape and once more started on our homeward voyage.

Mr and Mrs Chloet's house in Wineberg outside Capetown (author's image)

The front drive of this house in 1899.

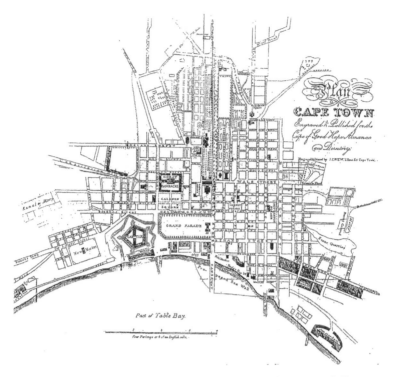

Plan of Cape Town in 1851. (from 'Cape of Good Hope almanac and directory' 1852)

Table Mountain, Cape Town, from out at sea (www.tourismcapetown.co.za)

Chapter 9

CAPE TOWN TO LONDON

Fifty-Five days at sea

Miriam's memoir contains no record of this part of the voyage.

The log book re-opened.

Friday 22nd February 1850

At noon got all my papers and all clear on shore. Came on board and weighed with finish of the S. Easter and made sail out of the bay.

Saturday 23rd February 1850

A.m strong breeze from S.E. and S.S.E. steering N.N.W. Rate of Sailing 9½ miles per hour. P.m breeze decreasing a little and cloudy.

On *Wednesday 27th February 1850* Alexander commented

P.m wind still at W.S.W. which is I should think very unusual in these latitudes as I have never before experienced such winds. Midnight winds light from the W.S.W.

Saturday 2nd March 1850

This weather is certainly unusual. We have had nothing but S.W. and Westerly winds since leaving Table Bay and the last day or two have been calm and light airs. At 6 p.m the Southampton alongside coming up fast. At 11 the Southampton alongside, gave him all the Cape hens.

I wonder if Harriet had been taken sometimes to look at the cape hens and would have been sad to see them go. I assume they may have been caught during some of the calms and could have been a tasty meal, or perhaps they were taken on board in Cape Town and were too much bother to keep.

Sunday 3ʳᵈ March 1850

Rate of sailing between 3 and 5½ miles per hour.

Tuesday 5ᵗʰ March 1850

A.m breeze increasing from the S.S.E. [At last, the wind had finally changed!]

P.m moderate trade wind and fine. All possible sail set. Rate of sailing 7 miles per hour. At 5.30 saw faintly thro' the haze the Island St Helena distant 22 miles and a ship supposed to be the Southampton apparently going in.

Seeing St Helena might have been of interest to those on board with memories of the exiled Napoleon.

Friday 8ᵗʰ March 1850

P.m light wind and fine. Unbent the main sail to repair.

I imagine Alexander was glad to be able to do it on a weekday, not a Sunday and with a light wind and fine weather so there could be no excuses for the crew to rebel this time!

Saturday 9ᵗʰ March 1850

P.m wind very light and has been so throughout the trade.

How frustrating when they were longing to get home.

Sunday 10ᵗʰ March 1850

P.m at 4 saw the Island of Ascension. distant 24 miles.

Thursday 14th March 1850

A.m light winds and fine, all possible sail set A strong current the last few days setting to the westward. P.m rate of sailing 5 miles per hour.

Monday 18th March 1850

A.m rate of sailing 2½ miles per hour. At daylight the Spanish ship Bella close to us. At 10 sent a boat overboard and got the news from St Helena and some tar and a few cheroots. At 2 the captain of the Spanish ship and a passenger came on board and dined and asked me to dine on board of their vessel tomorrow it being the birthday of the owner, to which I consented if circumstances would permit, tho' I thought there would be very little chance of doing so. Midnight light breezes and fine.

Perhaps Miriam would have met these two guests and enjoyed some socialising. I doubt if she or Alexander spoke Spanish but maybe there was someone who was able to translate. Perhaps they used a smattering of several languages and mimed!

Tuesday 19th March 1850

A.m light winds and fine. Lying North. Rate of sailing 3 miles per hour. Daylight the Spanish ship on the weather quarter. At 10 excused myself [by signal] not dining with him.

No reason was given for this, but perhaps Alexander did not like to leave the ship and his family or else he thought they had done enough socialising!

Saturday 23rd March 1850

P.m moderate and fine. Rate of sailing 7½ miles per hour. At daylight nothing in sight from the mast head. Employed cleaning ship.

Monday 25th March 1850

At daylight a Barque in sight on the weather bow about 5 miles distant. At 8.15 spoke the Barque Elinor from Barnsley belonging to Liverpool left St Helena on March 1st.

Rate of sailing 7 miles per hour.

Saturday 30th March 1850

A.m employed painting ship.

Perhaps Alexander wanted to make sure the *Charlotte Jane* arrived back looking spic and span, to impress her owners and also to be ready for the next voyage.

Sunday 31st March

A.m light airs and calms. Rate of sailing between 1½ to 2 miles per hour. P.m light winds but increasing towards evening. Rate of sailing 5 to 7½ miles per hour. Midnight almost calm.

Tuesday 2nd April 1850

A.m strong breezes at S.S.W. Rate of sailing 8 miles per hour. At 11 strong breezes and squally with rain. In all stud sails. Lower stud sail split and main royal, sent down royal yard. Noon. Heavy squalls with rain, in top gall sail. No observations for Latitude or longitude. Barque in sight on the larboard bow steering the same way and a barque on the lee beam also standing to the North East. P.m strong breezes. Unbent the main topsail and top gall sail and bent the best ones. At 10 violent squalls with rain. Split the jib. The fore sheet gave way. Split the fore sail, also split main topmast stay sail. I must here remark that this was principally caused by the sailor at the helm bringing the ship 4 points windward of her course. The man's name is Maulden. Double reefed the topsail and unbent the foresail. Midnight hard gales.

Wednesday 3rd April 1850

A.m hard gales. with a heavy sea. Ship labouring and straining a good deal. Rate of sailing 5½ to 7½ miles per hour. At daylight bent and reefed the best foresail and set it, bent another jib. Blowing very hard. with violent squalls. Ship labouring and straining a great deal and shipping a good deal of water. Midnight tremendous squalls. In jib and main sail and kept off during the height of it.

This would have been very tough for all the crew as well as Miriam and Helen. Keeping Harriet and baby Alexander inside for such long periods and safe from being thrown about from the rolling and plunging of the ship would have been tedious and worrying, especially if they were feeling sea sick. Harriet would have been nearly two and a half, a demanding age, and Alexander nine months and probably crawling all over the place. I wonder if they sang songs and nursery rhymes.to keep themselves amused.

It is interesting that singing is not mentioned in either the log book or the memoir. I have always imagined sailors singing shanties while on duty. Miriam mentioned the Lascars singing to a guitar but I felt quite disappointed not to have heard about any other songs.

Thursday 4th April 1850

A.m fresh gales with very violent squalls about every 2 hours, accompanied by rain. No keeping the ship off in one of these. The same man Maulden brought the ship by the Lee. He was sent away from the wheel with strict injunctions not to allow him to go there again at any time. Daylight more moderate found the clue ropes of the fore top sail gone. Clued it up and repaired it and set the main sail, reefed it and the jib. A barque in sight on the weather bow P.m more moderate. Let out some of the reefs.

[Alexander had scrawled two lines vertically at the side of the page over this entry, but it is smudged and tantalisingly unreadable!]

I dread to think what it would have been like to be up and down the rigging during such gales having to constantly attend to the sails. It is terrifying enough to contemplate in daylight but even more so in total darkness. I imagine the crew were all getting worn out. There is no mention in the log or the memoir of any death or serious injury.

Saturday 6ᵗʰ April 1850

A.m strong gales. Rate of sailing 8½ miles per hour. At daylight same weather with rain. A Dutch ship in sight to windward. P.m violent squalls with heavy rain. A Barque in sight close, the Princess Aurora. Altered the course to pass to the Southward of Flores Island. At 6 p.m furled the main top gall sail and treble reefed the main top sail and set the reefed main sail. Midnight Strong gales.

Sunday 7ᵗʰ April 1850

A.m strong gales Rate of sailing 8½ to 9 miles per hour. Observed the water become smooth and violent gusts of wind.

[I am unable to read this section but I gather that another sail was unbent and had to be repaired and bent].

6 p.m light breeze with thick hazy weather.

Monday 8ᵗʰ April 1850

A.m unbent the main sail to repair.

Tuesday 9ᵗʰ April 1850

An increasing breeze. At 6.30 p.m the sheeting of the lower stud sail gave way hauled it in at 7, the main top gall ---- gave way, Gale increasing ---- two reefs in the main top sail. Reefed and stowed the main sail. Strong gale and squally with rain. At 8.30 during a heavy squall both the main topsail sheet whips gave way. Clued the sail up in time to save it from being split. Lash another reef in it and set it. Midnight hard gales with heavy squalls.

Alexander was running out of ink and his pen was making odd splodges in amongst his fading writing! I imagine everyone was running out of energy at this long last haul to get home.

Wednesday 10th April 1850

Ship labouring and straining a good deal during the night, strong gales. But nothing making the course good. Saw everything clear for a hard gale.

Midnight gale increasing.

Yet another gale on the way!

Thursday 11th April 1850

A.m hard gales with violent squalls. At 4 the gale at its height with dark raining weather. At 8 very much more moderate. Wind more to the Northward and glass rising, Midnight moderate and fine.

Saturday 13th April 1850

At 10 a.m the man at the helm allowed the ship to fly up on the wind. Carried away foretop mast and top gall stud sail ----. Cleared away the wrecks and sent up one of the main top mast sheet sail-----. P.m Altered the course for the Lizard.

The log book ended at this point. Once again Alexander ceased writing the log, as he had near Hong Kong. Maybe he had completely run out of ink and so could not write another word. There is no record of which port they disembarked, although Miriam was definite that it was London. What fearfully difficult and exhausting final days they experienced as catastrophes piled one on top of another, and they floundered about with ferocious gales, split sails, and broken masts.

Miriam wrote:

We arrived in due time at London experiencing heavy contrary gales in the channel. As nearly all our clothes were worn out and our stores running short, we were very pleased once more to be at home in Old England.

One can imagine the relief, delight and immense sense of achievement they must have felt as they disembarked from the *Charlotte Jane* after nearly two years at sea. We have no idea whether any of the family were able to meet them off the ship to celebrate their safe return but it is unlikely as communications were limited and it would have been difficult to know exactly when a ship might arrive.

I wonder where Miriam and Alexander went to start life again in England. Perhaps they went to Walworth Terrace where they had started their married life or they may, at first, have gone to stay with Miriam's parents.

Settling back and adjusting to life on land probably took a while. As well as the thrill of being home there would be all the practicalities to attend to, such as finding a house suitable for two small children and perhaps a growing family and especially one in which Miriam could feel safe when Alexander would be away at sea. Harriet and Alexander Macclesfield would find living in a house quite strange. Not having sailors around all the time would have felt very odd. I wonder if Helen stayed on with the family or if Miriam decided to get rid of her, in which case the children might have missed her a great deal. Or, of course Helen may have been eagerly looking forward to being with her own family again and then finding work elsewhere.

Captain Lawrence's sea desk (collection of the author) with his log book on the raised writing board in the open top drawer, left, and in the drawer one of Miriam's letters before folding to send home, right.

Chapter 10

AFTERWARDS

Four months after returning from her Maiden voyage the *Charlotte Jane* once again set sail on 7th September 1850 this time from Plymouth to Port Lyttleton, New Zealand with Alexander Lawrence in command. She was in the company of three other ships the *George Seymour*, the *Randolph,* and the *Cressy*. They were all carrying early colonists and emigrants to a new settlement at Lyttleton on the South Island of New Zealand, chartered by the Canterbury Association.

The ships competed against each other to be the first to arrive and it was the *Charlotte Jane* that achieved this. There is a letter of gratitude from the passengers, a few diaries of the voyage, and other memorabilia kept in the Christchurch Museum in Canterbury New Zealand where the *Charlotte Jane* and Captain Lawrence are held in high esteem, being part of the early settlers' history.

By 1854 Alexander was in Command of the *Orient*, also owned by the Anderson Company. We do not know who had taken command of the *Charlotte Jane.*

In amongst Miriam's effects, we found a newspaper cutting of an obituary for Alexander but the name of the newspaper has been cut off! I include it here.

The late Captain Lawrence.

Mr Alexander Lawrence of Clyde House, Thurlow Road, for many year's resident in Hampstead, and one of the officers of Trinity

Presbyterian Church, died rather suddenly at his residence on Sunday last, after a very short illness.

Mr Lawrence began a sailor's career at a very early age, and was afterwards for many years in command of a vessel, The *Orient* in the Australian Trade. It was this vessel that gave the name to the well-known *Orient* line of steamers. The greater number of these vessels were chartered by the government during the Crimean war, and they did good service in conveying stores to the army and in carrying the wounded to Scutari. The vessel commanded by Captain Lawrence was one of the few that safely escaped from the terrible tempest in the Black Sea in November 1854.

During the many voyages taken by Captain Lawrence, he met with only one serious calamity, and that took place on his last journey. When near St Helena a fire broke out on board his vessel, and for three days the destructive element had to be battled with, and the lives of all in the vessel were placed in great jeopardy. But so heroic and persistent were the efforts of Captain Lawrence and his officers that the fire was kept down and the vessel ultimately run safely into harbour, but not before a portion of the interior of her hull had become a charred mass. Captain Lawrence's gallant conduct on this occasion was so much appreciated that it led to a very handsome testimonial being presented to him by the underwriters at Lloyds.

For more than a quarter of a century after retiring from active service as a commander Captain Lawrence carried on the business of an Australian merchant, and for some years past his son has been engaged with him in the same business.

Captain Lawrence, who was of a most genial disposition, but had the faculty of winning and attaching friends all through his life, and was trusted and honoured by all who had the pleasure of his acquaintance. He had a large circle of friends amongst city men and colonial merchants. By the circle of Presbyterians in Hampstead he will be greatly missed.

The interment took place on Thursday at Highgate cemetery and was witnessed by a large number of the relatives and friends of the deceased. The arrangements were under the superintendence of Mr Richard Clowser, of High Street. The Cortege comprised the car, and seventeen private carriages amongst them being the Carriages of Mr H.M. Matheson, James Matheson, Dr F. Anderson, Sir Edward Blythie, Mr Hay, Mr Tinline and Mr Johnston. The coffin was covered with wreaths, a very choice one being contributed by the office bearers of the Presbyterian Church. The coffin was a polished oak, with a brass plate bearing the following inscription; 'Alexander Lawrence born 31st May 1813, died 13th June 1886.' Rev J. Matheson, for many years the loved and esteemed minister of the Presbyterian Church conducted the funeral service, during which two hymns were sung, one of them 'Oh eyes that are weary' being an especial favourite of the deceased. Some hundreds of people attended the funeral.

Miriam and Alexander had eleven children, nine daughters and two sons. One daughter died in infancy, another died at sea aged about 13 months. Another daughter died aged about 11 years old. We do not have a cause of death. When travelling in the USA in 1884 Miriam and Alexander visited Salt Lake City and the Mormon Church. In her journal of that date, she mentioned that she had been thinking of her lost little ones.

Harriet married Matthew Little a widower in 1872 who already had two children from his first marriage. He had lived in Singapore for several years and was a merchant. He and Harriet visited Singapore in 1876. They had several children and lived next door to Miriam and Alexander in Thurlow Road, Hampstead.

Alexander Macclesfield as already mentioned in the obituary joined his father's business. He married Mary Isabella Hamilton in 1882. We have several delightful letters written by her to Alexander Macclesfield's youngest sister, Emily. They were obviously very close friends. Alexander Macclesfield was hit by tragedy. In 1884 his baby daughter Mona, died probably from whooping cough. Two years later his father died and the following year 1887 Isabella died leaving a baby boy aged one month old, called Mervyn; an eighteen-month, baby girl called Gladys and a boy called Hamilton aged three years old.

Sometime later, I do not know exactly when, Alexander Macclesfield went to live and work in South Africa leaving his children in the care of his youngest sister Emily. The family story is that she turned down an offer of marriage in order to devote herself entirely to their care. She remained unmarried throughout her life and was greatly loved by all the family. My husband, Hal met her when he was a very small child but remembers her with affection.

Alexander Macclesfield returned from South Africa some years later. He died in London in 1934.The Company Lawrence and Son was probably disbanded around the time he went to South Africa. It did not prosper as it is thought the Lawrence family were a bit old fashioned and would have nothing to do with steamships! Gradually sailing ships became unable to compete with steam especially after the Suez Canal was built.

Miriam lived in Hampstead for the rest of her life with Emily. I think they became less well off as the years went by. She had a large number of grandchildren in this country as well as in Canada. Her youngest child William Stanley, known as Ben emigrated to Canada where he married and had a large family. Her two grandsons Hamilton and Mervyn Lawrence likewise followed a few years after.

I like to think that all Miriam's children and grandchildren may have enjoyed hearing and or reading her memoir.

Miriam died in 1913.

Of Helen and Dr Jamieson nothing further is known.

Settlers arriving at Port Lyttleton, South Island, New Zealand,
after *Charlotte Jane*'s second voyage in 1850

Charlotte Jane lying off Port Lyttleton in 1850. (This image is part of a photograph of a picture,
photographed by Robin Vaughan Francis Smith of Robin Smith Photography Ltd)

GLOSSARY

Aft. An abbreviation of abaft, meaning the hinder part of the ship or that nearest the stern.

After-hold. The area behind the main mast towards the back in the lower part of the ship.

Anchor. A large and heavy instrument which when dropped to the bottom of the sea holds the ship fast.

Anchorage. A place suitable for a ship to anchor.

Bower anchors. Those at the bows and often used. The bower anchor on the starboard side is called the 'best' and that on the larboard side 'small'.

Beams. Strong transverse pieces of timber stretching across the ship from one side to the other.

Beam-ends. When a ship has heeled over so far that her beams are almost vertical.

Bend a sail. To extend or make it fast to its proper yard or stay.

To unbend a sail. To remove the sails from their yards and stays.

Below. The area below deck.

Boom. A spar to which the foot of a sail is fastened to control its position.

Bulwarks. The planking or woodwork round a vessel above deck, fixed to upright pieces of wood placed at intervals along the sides of the ship.

Cables length is 100 fathoms. [A fathom is 6 feet.]

Ceedies. I am not sure if I have read this word right. Porters about the wharfs in Bombay.

Carried away. Broken off.

Chronometer. A clock that keeps accurate time on board ship it enables mariners to calculate longitude.

Cooper. A person who makes or repairs barrels and casks.

Cuddy. A cabin under the poop deck for the Captain and his guests.

Daguerreotype. A type of early photograph produced on chemically treated silver.

Dog-shores. Two long square blocks of timber placed to prevent a newly built ship from slipping into the water.

Fitter and turner. A person who fits and adapts things. A turner is a person who turns wood.

Fathom. Six feet.

Fore chains. Chains are broad pieces of wood bolted to the outside of a vessel used for spreading the lower rigging. Designated fore, main and mizen.

Furling. Rolling up and binding sails to the yards.

Garry A cart for two people, drawn by a horse with a driver who runs along beside, known as a Garry Walla.

The glass. The telescope.

The gig. A ship's boat adapted for rowing and sailing.

A Hand. Means a member of the crew.

Hatch. An opening in the deck of a ship, such as, above the hold.

Head sea. The name given to the waves when they oppose the ship's course, as the ship must rise over, or cut through each one. Sometimes they are steep, quick and irregular, so that a ship is caught by a second before she has recovered from the first. These render her wet and uneasy.

Halyards. The rope or tackle used to hoist or lower a sail upon its yards, gaff or stays.

Hatches. Half doors.

Holystone. A sandstone for scrubbing decks. Originally so called because it was used on Sundays or obtained by plundering churchyards of their tombstones. Or because the seamen have to kneel to scrub.

Hull down. When a ship is seen at such a distance that only her masts and sails are to be seen.

Jalousies. Shutters.

Jib. Triangular sail set in front of the foremast.

Labouring. When a ship is pitching and rolling in a turbulent sea, by which the masts and even the hull, are greatly endangered.

Larboard and starboard. Larboard is the left side of the ship when facing the bow. Starboard means the right side of the ship. (Derived from Italian Questa borda meaning this side, and quella borda meaning that side.) The similarity of these words caused many mistakes and so larboard was eventually changed to port.

Lascars. Sailors from India and South East Asia.

Latitude. In wide terms, the extent of the earth from one pole to the other, but strictly it is the distance of any place from the equator in degrees and their parts.

Latitude by observation. Latitude determined by observations of the sun, stars or moon.

Latitude by account. That estimated by the log-board and the last determined observation.

Log Board. Two boards shutting together like a book, and divided into several columns, in which to record, through the hours of the day and night, the direction of the wind and the course of the ship, with all the material occurrences, together with the latitude by observation. From this table the officers record the ship's way, and compile their journals. The whole being written by the mate of the watch with chalk is rubbed out every day at noon. A slate more generally used.

Longitude. Is an arc of the equator, or any parallel of latitude, contained between the meridian of a place and that of Greenwich, or any first meridian. These arcs being similar, are expressed, by the same number of degrees and miles, though the absolute distance on the earth's surface decreases as the latitude increases. East Longitude extends 180 degrees to the right when looking North, and West longitude as many to the left of the first meridian.

Mess. To eat, drink and associate with one another.

Mizen top mast head. The Mizen mast is the aftermost mast of a ship. The Topmast is the second division of a mast above deck and the head means the upper part.

Oakum. Untwisted old rope used in caulking seams to stop leaks. Also used in making twice used rope.

On end. To get the topmast on end means to set it properly in its place in an upright position.

Pilot. An experienced person usually taken out in a small boat to board a visiting vessel. He takes responsibility to steer it safely through difficult passages such as in and out of harbours. Along hazardous coastlines, and through intricate channels, because he knows that particular district very well. Having completed his task, he returns to his own boat.

Pitch. A boiled mixture of tar and coarse resin, used hot with oakum in caulking the ship filling in the gaps between planks on the deck.

Pitching. The plunging of a ship's head in a seaway; the vertical vibration which her length makes about her centre of gravity; a very straining motion.

Poop. A deck built above the quarter deck at the stern of the ship.

Quarter deck. The part of the upper deck that is towards the back of the ship behind the main mast.

A Sampan. A small flat-bottomed boat with oars used for passengers by the Chinese. Often has a roof.

A Sawyer. A person who saws wood for a living.

Sedan chair. A semi-enclosed chair on poles carried by men back and front.

Serang. Head of a Lascar crew

Snug. Under proper sail to meet a gale.

Spar. The general term for all masts, yards, booms etc.

Squalls. Sudden gusts of wind, frequently occurring due to interruption and reverberation of the wind from high mountains. Frequent in the Mediterranean, particularly in the Levant. A black squall is a gust of wind with a dark cloud and generally heavy rain. A white squall is a fierce and dangerous gust of wind which occurs in fine weather without any warning except a white foam on the surface of the sea and a thin haze, followed by very heavy rain. It is very dangerous if the high sails are flying as they can be torn off in the sudden wind.

Stern. The back part of the ship.

Tender. A ship being tender is inclined to lean over and in danger of overturning due to insufficient ballast or unbalanced cargo.

To fly up in the wind. When a ship's head comes suddenly to windward, by carelessness of the helmsman.

Top sails. The second sails above the decks, extending across the top masts, by the topsail yards above and by the lower yards.

Trade winds. Currents of air moving from about the 30th degree of latitude towards the equator. The diurnal motion of the earth makes them incline from the eastward, so that in the northern hemisphere they are from the N.E. and in the Southern hemisphere from the S.E. Their geographical position in latitude varies with the declination of the sun. In some parts of the world, such as the Bay of Bengal and the China Sea, the action of the sun on the neighbouring land has the power of reversing the trades; the winds there are called monsoons.

Tropics. Two imaginary lines upon the globe, or lesser circles of the sphere, parallel to the equator, at 23½ degrees distance on each side of it; they touch the ecliptic at its greatest distances from the equator, and from the boundaries of the sun's declination, north and south.

Tween decks. Under the gun deck, where the sailors usually mess.

Whirlwind. A revolving current of wind of small diameter that rises suddenly, but is soon past.

Windward. Of or in the direction from which wind blows.

Worsted thread. Woollen thread.

Yards. The horizontal spars to which the sails are attached.

Yardarm. The outer end of a ships yard.

BIBLIOGRAPHY

Before the Mast in the Clippers. The Diaries of Charles A. Abbey, 1856 to 1860. Harpur Allen Gosnell.

SS Great Britain. Brunell's Ship, Her Voyages, Passengers and Crew, Helen Doe. Amberley.

Sea Stories, New Writing from the National Maritime Museum.

Married and Gone to New Zealand, Alison Drummond. First Published 1960. Paul. London.

Hen Frigates. Wives of Merchant Captains under Sail, Joan Druett. Simon & Schuster;

The Commanding Sea. Six Voyages of Discovery, Clare Francis and Warren Tute. Book Club Associates. London.

The Voyage of the Caroline, by Rosalie Hare 1827–28. Edited by Ida Lee. Longmans.

I Saw a Ship a 'Sailing, Mary Hay. London. Her Majesty's Stationery Office.

The Hong Kong Guide. 1839, With an Introduction by H.J. Letherbridge. Hong Kong Oxford University.

A Lady's Captivity Among Chinese Pirates, Fanny Loviot. National Maritime Museum.

The Adventure of Sail 1520 – 1914, Donald Macintyre. Ferndale Editions London.

Erebus. The Story of a Ship, Michael Palin. Penguin Random House UK.

Memoirs of a Seafaring Life. The Narrative of William Spavens, Edited and Introduced by N. A. M. Rodger. Printed by the Bath Press, in the County of Somerset, for the Members of the Folio Society. MM.

A personal Anthology of Ships and Men, Compiled by Alan Villiers. Newnes: London.

Square-Rigged Ships. An Introduction, Alan Villiers. National Maritime Museum.

My Ancestor was a Merchant Seaman, Christopher T. and Michael J. Watts. Society of Genealogists Enterprises Ltd.

Clipper Ships. The Seafarers, By A.B.C. Whipple and the Editors of Time-Life Books.

The Loss of the Criccieth Castle. A True Account of Heroism and Survival, By Cathy Woodhead. Published in 2012 by Delfryn Publications, Delfryn, Borth-Y- Gest, Porthmadog, Gwynedd LL 49 9TW. UK.

The Social Life of Opium in China. Zheng Yangwen 2005. Cambridge University Press.

Lightning Source UK Ltd.
Milton Keynes UK
UKHW050944061121
393452UK00004B/45